GEOFFREY FLETCHER'S LONDON

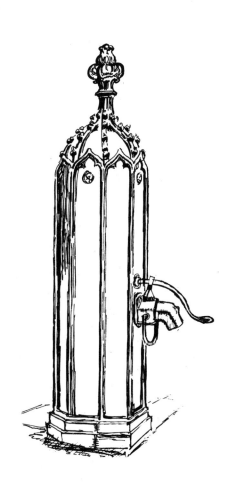

BOOKS BY GEOFFREY FLETCHER

Town's Eye View

The London Nobody Knows

City Sights

London Overlooked

Pearly Kingdom

Down Among the Meths Men

London's River

London's Pavement Pounders

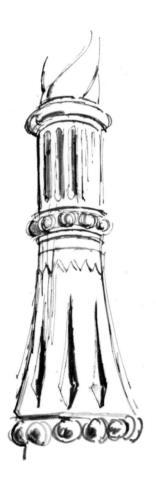

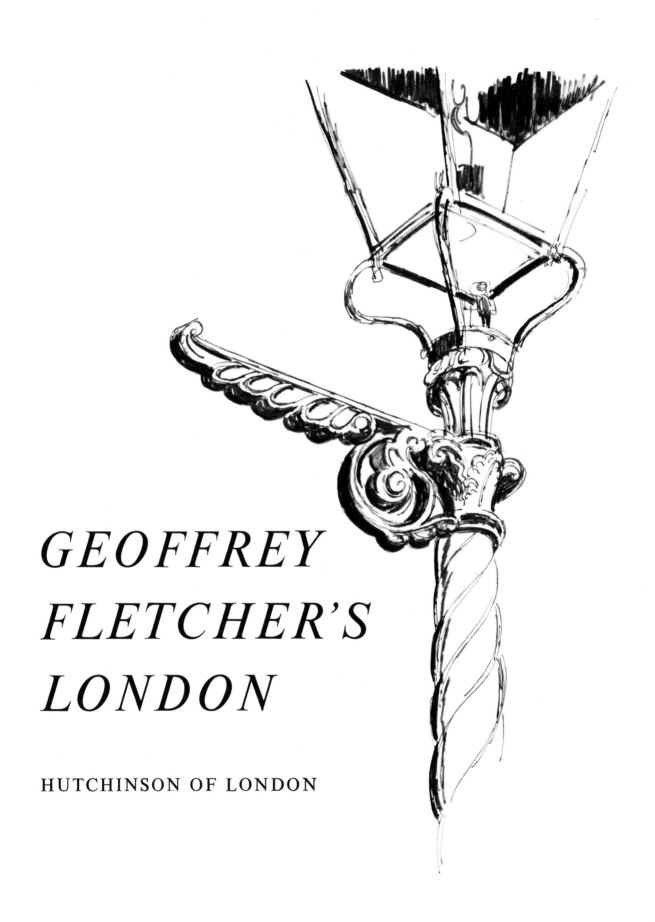

GEOFFREY FLETCHER'S LONDON

HUTCHINSON OF LONDON

HUTCHINSON & CO (*Publishers*) LTD
178–202 Great Portland Street, London W1

London Melbourne Sydney
Auckland Bombay Toronto
Johannesburg New York

First published 1968

*Printed in Great Britain by offset litho at
Taylor Garnett Evans & Co Ltd, Watford,
Herts and bound by Wm. Brendon of
Tiptree, Essex*

Design by Rosemary Harley

09 088610 0

Contents

A number of paragraphs in this book and a few of the illustrations have appeared in *The Daily Telegraph*, to which I have pleasure in making the usual acknowledgements.

This book is dedicated
to the memory of my dog
RAGS
May 1953–July 1967
my companion on many journeys
in Geoffrey Fletcher's London

Is life a boon?
If so, it must befall
That Death, when'er he call,
Must call too soon.

I

'Those Wonderful People out there in the Dark'

———— * ————

I CANNOT REMEMBER A TIME when I was not a cinema addict. The years yawn—as did my captive audiences of mutinous adults—between the magic lantern shows (*John Gilpin* and *The Curfew Shall Not Ring Tonight*) with which I got myself hooked, and the James Mason film recently made from my book *The London Nobody knows*. Between them are too many epics they said could never be brought to the silver screen, too many all singing, all musical, sexy spectaculars—too many (far too many) super special pictures of the year.

Yet, my pleasure in the cinema has declined as the motion picture has advanced technically and artistically, and I believe the reason is that going to the flicks is no longer the fun it used to be in days of old when Hollywood knights were bold and were usually named Fairbanks or Flynn. It was good to watch the commissionaire—a no-nonsense figure who had no doubt been a warrant officer on the Western Front—spray Flit during the interval, good to watch *The Perils of Pauline* who was still going the rounds of the flea pits when I began my apprenticeship and better still to have a pianist play 'Hearts and Flowers' during the big love scene and rattle her coconuts like castanets when the lone stranger rode into town.

The rot set in with the talkies. I didn't realise this when I went to see *The Singing Fool* (how the customers sobbed—not a dry eye in the house) but I do now. In fact, I have never accepted them. I never accepted Mickey Mouse, if it comes to that: I always preferred Felix. In a word, I have no high falutin' ideas about the cinema. I don't regard it as an art form: it is to me simply an entertainment for the middle and lower classes, just that and nothing else, and I believe that the more the cinema has grown from its celluloid roots in the old fairground booths and temperance halls, the less interesting it has become. It is the same with cars: one is prepared to accept, though with reservations, the productions of the 1930s, but a true connoisseur must turn to the earlier years—the Golden Age—for real satisfaction. Therefore my hope for the cinema is for a return to its earlier days, or at least to an eclectic period somewhere between the nickelodeon era and the talkies, and to stay there, in black and white, and silent.

It seems to me remarkable how, in endeavours where artistic feeling is associated with technical or inventive skill, the most satisfactory point of achievement

9

is quickly reached. The history of photography itself is a proof of this assertion, the pioneers like Fox-Talbot leaving little for the later men to do, except to simplify and rationalise processes, but all that mattered artistically had been said and done. The cinema tried too hard, did too much and took itself too seriously. To me, cinema-going is a period undertaking: it is old-fashioned to go to the flicks, and we ought to make the most of it. For instance, modern audiences are wrongly dressed for most of the existing cinemas—in some cases ludicrously so—and this want of harmony between architecture and audience limits one's enjoyment. As many of the cinemas lucky enough to survive are now too historically important to alter, apart from the expense and absurdity of doing so, the only way to correct the imbalance is to create a period clientèle—a genuinely period audience, not a collection of fools in fancy dress, such as we see at the feeble attempts to revive the music halls, but composed of people who genuinely reject the present age, preferring the 1930s or the '20s or others, like myself, who wish they had lived before the Great War.

Cinema-going is to me an experience *in the round*. I am not content to sit passively in my seat, eyeing the film: the bags of crisps, the adverts for prams and hairdressers, the choc-ices, the lavatory regularly disinfected with Jeyes, even the clip-on bow-tie of the manager, all contribute to the business in hand. The film is only part of the whole. Now, at last, a society has been formed to study and record the cinemas. The society will seek to safeguard not only the humble picture theatres of the 1920s and earlier, but also the huge, magnificent cinemas of the 1930s like the Astoria at Finsbury Park, which has Moorish battlements over the proscenium, its namesake at Brixton, and the Granada, Tooting. London has still a good collection of these mammoth 3,000 seaters, though they are gradually being demolished or turned into supermarkets or bingo joints. See, for instance, the Gaumont State at Kilburn—still in existence, though the great times have gone. The Gaumont State was the last word in super cinemas de luxe in the 1930s; before the war you got a marathon programme lasting about four hours, with a stage show thrown in. In the same visit, you can take in The Grange, Kilburn High Road, one of the earlier luxury cinemas that superannuated my beloved flea pits.

When these de luxe affairs first opened, they provided an antidote to the depression era—just as the gin palace provided an escape from the realities of the mean streets in the middle of the last century. Some had fountains playing in the foyers. Many had twenty-piece orchestras or vast organs. (As I write the words, I see the Wurlitzers in my mind's eye endlessly rising from the depths below stage as they played themselves in, in rainbow-hued spotlights and elaborate lighting effects with clouds scudding across the ceilings, and the maestros themselves, dream merchants the lot of them, smiling your cares away as they sat at the console—they were always smiling under their little moustaches.) Besides all this, there was heaven, too, in the shape of talent spotting contests, held by warm hearted manag-

ers, with lots of huha in the local press and maybe a visit to a film studio and lunch with a star. . . . We never realised in those days that we would never have it so good again. Now we are grown old—even the young are old—sophisticated, worldly-wise, and film stars would hardly know an orgy from a revivalist meeting. Or I suppost not.

As an antidote to changed times, I recently visited the Biograph near Victoria, the first cinema to be built as such in England. At one time there was a rival concern in the area, formerly the Vauxhall Music Hall, and it retained its much patronised bar, the whole set-up being richly South London and the clientèle friendly and family-like. The Biograph has now become monumental, and the habit of going to it an institution among connoisseurs. But the locals of Vauxhall and Pimlico have been doing this for years, handing on the practice from father to son. As a result, the audience, always (I believe) predominantly male, projects an atmosphere of belonging, almost as if they had shares in the place. Westerns are a staple diet, together with highly-flavoured items such as *I married a Were-wolf*, which was being screened on my last visit. The only concession to today's conditions is in the recent tarting up of the exterior. The interior, with its 1905 projection box, remains intact.

The audience, well laced with old-aged pensioners, is particularly rich in the afternoons. Apathy overtakes many of the customers in a way only paralleled in my experience by Collins's, Islington. Some of the customers fall asleep, while others eat sandwiches or talk to themselves. On my last visit a mild nut case spent the first half of the programme swatting an imaginary fly with a magazine, and the second half viewing the screen through the same magazine rolled up into a telescope—the Nelson touch. This, though a great joy to me, would be likely to prove less attractive to his neighbours—or so I fancied—but nobody minded in the least. People are easy at the Bio. They watch a teenage werewolf with the same complacency with which they once followed the fortunes of the world's sweetheart, Mary Pickford, and a monster from ten thousand fathoms doesn't give them a moment's discomfort.

Such cinemas have their memorial in the Peter Sellers film, *The Smallest Show on Earth*—a production that had the opposite effect on me to the one the makers presumably intended. Besides the few 'fleapits', there are the smaller cinemas of the 1930s remaining more or less in quantity in the London suburbs. As economic factors and precious little else govern the fate of picture houses, these are the ones most likely to meet the changed conditions, and so have better prospects for survival. The Odeon, Haverstock Hill, is a typical example: no doubt someone will include it in time in a learned analysis, 'The Smaller Urban Cinema of the Late Jazz Age'. If this book is ever undertaken, I present its author with the pick of my bunch—the Egyptian cinema in Essex Road, Islington (previous page and opposite). It is one of my favourite London cinemas—one that ought to have a preservation order put on it. Huge lotus-Bud capitals support a cornice (polychromatically coloured, like the capitals) that might not have been considered a bad effort at Edfu, of which the temple of Horus might have been the inspiration for the façade (it is, of course, *all* façade—the place being incorrigibly 1930 in its hindquarters). Another possible source is the Ptolemaic temple of Isis at Philae—this is a better guess, perhaps, for the foyer of the cinema is Greek, which only goes to prove that the Ptolemies were still influential even in the Jazz Age. One wonders what Isis and Osiris would have made of the Hollywood deities to whom the temple was dedicated, not to mention the laundry-lugging old girls of Islington and their iced-lolly-licking grandchildren who pass across the forecourt. . . .

One thing is certain. This cinema has been a great comfort to me since the untimely and unfeeling stripping of the Egyptian decorations from the Black Cat factory—now only a ghost of its former self—at Mornington Crescent. Adelaide House, erected in the early 1920s on the N.E. corner of London Bridge (completely dominating the church of St Magnus the Martyr), is too gross, somehow, for the collector of architectural fantasies. But the Essex Road Egyptian is a light pastiche that unashamedly announces itself as belonging to the period of the man about town, the well-dressed racketeers, the international vamps and the

Queen Mary. Adelaide House is ponderous, monolithic. It is perhaps best described as Thameside C. B. de Mille.

Plans and elevations for 'Picture Theatres', as they called them in the age of innocence, appear surprisingly early in the architectural journals: the more ambitious ones with either the trimmings of Edwardian Baroque—swags, egg and dart mouldings, elliptical windows (one of the commissionaire's jobs was to pull the blinds down over the windows with a long pole) and dumpy columns— or those of late Art Nouveau—its stiffer, least interesting phase. Cheaper flick palaces approximated to the styles of their near relatives, the billiard halls and skating rinks. A good number of these remain, as I have said, mostly in the old, unfashionable (then as now) London suburbs, such as Hackney, Balham and Clapham. For some reason, perhaps because of the lingering influence of music

14

hall and theatre architecture, allied to Edwardian Baroque, classic details became general. One of the last examples of this is the Villa Cross cinema in Birmingham, with sculptured medallions on the walls of the auditorium. Occasionally a cinema owner would tempt his patrons (almost always working class at this time) with an exotic—like the Indian style picture palace in Upper Richmond Road or the Moorish specimen in Portsmouth.

Of the standard classic, one of my favourites is the Rex on Islington Green (opposite). The best time to see it is on a winter afternoon when the red and blue neon lights come on to gladden the hearts of the dead-end kids and dim old men and women who have been hanging round the entrance for ages in anticipation. As opening time draws near the suspense becomes unbearable. They can hardly wait to pass through the portals into a more abundant life. The bright lights beckon to them through the bare black trees of the Green. You watch the old girls as they totter in these cinemas with their heavy bags, and the mumbling old men in their mufflers, and wonder if they are aware that, though the cinema is the most realistic artistic medium that man has yet devised, they are not in fact in search of reality, for reality is the one thing they cannot stand. What they want are the old myths acted out, unchanged in essentials, year after year. They want goodies and baddies, sex and spectacle, hokum and corn, just as they have always done. They are admitted to these things with an omniscience once permitted only to the Gods. But these old Chelsea figures, these dwellers in Clapham or Battersea Rise, are more awe inspiring than the Gods of old time. What antique God would be impassive enough to eat a choc ice while watching Moses break the tablets of the Law? Sometimes, even today, in the fleapits, one of their number, more impressionable than the rest, will rouse himself from lethargy to shout advice, as of old time, to the hero on the screen. But the shadow play, like life itself, remorselessly pursues its appointed course to the final fade-out, heedless of interruptions, deaf to the cries of 'Watch him—he's got a gun' that come from the customers in the stalls, 'those wonderful people', as Norma Desmond called them, 'those wonderful people out there in the dark.'

'gothic' streetlamp
Mount Pleasant
SB Whitely

II

On Foot in Finsbury

———— * ————

FINSBURY, now absorbed administratively in Islington (just as at an earlier period the Borough itself absorbed Clerkenwell), had among its many attractions a couple of star items of peculiar charm. These were Pluto, the tea and coffee brewing gas lamp (on the open space in Rosebery Avenue at the Exmouth Street end), and the privately owned lavatory, run as a profit-making concern until it

16

went 'public' under the local council. Pluto, although well before my time, was pure Fletcher's London. He was inaugurated on February 7th, 1899, the Pluto Hot Water Syndicate having been permitted by the Clerkenwell Vestry to instal him on the site. There is a faded photograph in Islington Library of the event, attended, as such things always were in those days, by a number of fierce-looking men in fur and velvet collars, walrus moustaches, silk hats and Derbys. Pluto supplied cold water free or a quart of boiling water for a halfpenny. Also for a halfpenny, this accommodating gas lamp supplied a cup of tea, coffee or cocoa: for picturesqueness—he had a marvellous lamp atop of him, decorated with a lace-like edge—and utility (not to speak of value), Pluto had his later imitators beaten hollow. There were other splendid lamps at this point—the junction of Farringdon Road and Rosebery Avenue—at this time, with the single-decker Kingsway and Aldwych trams thrown in. Though these have all vanished, there remains a small collection of delightful, fancifully designed Gothic gas lamps (opposite) in the street round Mount Pleasant. Take a 171 bus from Chancery Lane, the more so as Clerkenwell, where the City clerks used to take themselves for a holiday, is of all the central London districts the least visited by tourists.

Begin by going down Mount Pleasant (wonderfully misnamed, for in the eighteenth century the mount was nothing more than a gigantic dust heap formed originally from the rubble cleared out of the City after the Great Fire). The old Phoenix Foundry and a row of eighteenth-century houses (one dated 1720) remain among the offices and warehouses, and there is a typical London local, the Apple Tree. The foundry, now empty, will eventually be demolished. The owners, Bowen & Company, who produced one of the early motor cars, 'The Bowen', in 1906— the engine and chassis being built entirely at their works—have now removed to Herne Hill, taking with them the delightful Coade stone emblem of the foundry— a somewhat cross-looking Phoenix arising from flames, mortars and cannonball.

From Mount Pleasant make a short detour into Farringdon Road, where the grey slabs of Victorian industrial flats of a wonderful meanness are intersected by alleys with names that remind you of the vanished rural charms of the area, which was at one time full of tea gardens, pleasaunces and minor spas—names like Vineyard Walk and Bowling Green Lane. Here are grocers and wine shops specialising in Italian foods and the cork shop of W. Plesents. You can buy any kind of cork here, or admire the fascinating arrangements in cork (which include models under glass shades) in the window for nothing.

Incidentally, though vines have long since vanished from Vineyard Walk, there are still votaries of Bacchus in the neighbourhood—I do not, of course, mean the Irish who get themselves airborne on St Patrick's night—for a short distance away, down King's Cross Road, are grape vines (probably over a century old, though their origin remains obscure) flourishing over the early nineteenth-century houses on the east side, an even more unlikely spot than Vineyard Walk. They were particularly luxuriant in 1947 and 1948, when I was at the Slade and used

17

to moon there after a meal at Reggioris or the B.R. and after staring in the windows of Bravington's. Bravington's used to have a slogan in those days:

Home again, Home again
Let us all sing
A sweet little girl
And a Bravington ring.

and this rather got on my mind: jingles always do.

Exmouth Market (opposite) is dominated by the church of the Holy Redeemer by J. D. Sedding, which gives you the feeling of being transported to Italy, a fantasy assisted by the considerable Italian population of the district, though they, in fact, have their own church, St Peter's (page 22), near Saffron Hill, facing the Northern end of Leather Lane. The Holy Redeemer has an interesting Italianate interior, with groined vaults, painted in pale blue, springing from a continuous entablature resting on huge Corinthian columns. There is a free-standing domed baldacchino, Florentine in inspiration, with red marble columns at the angles. The church has been recently cleaned and redecorated with the result that the huge columns stand out dramatically against lemon walls—this, the gilded statues of the ciborium, the silver candle-sticks and the stations of the cross make it hard to realize that the cabbages and cauliflowers, bananas, brussels and budgie foods of Exmouth Market are pressing close outside. The market is primarily eating, drinking and domestic: junk stalls are not its strong point: nonetheless, it is one of the most attractive of the North London street markets, one to be savoured slowly from end to end. At Mrs Paris's shellfish stall at the very beginning of the market—near to the site of the vanished Pluto lamp—you can indulge in some of the largest prawns and most succulent mussels in London, aided and abetted if you wish by the humble, long-lasting whelk or the aristocratic, glorious oyster.

Farther down on the same side, if your taste inclines to the jellied eel, is the emporium I illustrate (page 20)—Manze's—a regular London establishment equipped with boxes like those of the old coffee houses for the private consumption of the delicacy. This shop is a twin to the one in Chapel Market, a mile or so up in Islington, recorded in the film *The London Nobody Knows*. The clientèle is almost interchangeable. Visit it and have a bash at sausages and mash or eels and mash. Note the curious combination of speed and detachment with which the bowls of jellied eels are emptied, listen to the conversation (always about the iniquities of wives or husbands or neighbours, or about illness and death) and marvel at the unchanged spirit of the real working-class Londoner, for this is a genuine honest-to-God Victorian experience you are having—make no mistake about it. Look out for the tired old women and old men with eyes as sad as those of a bloodhound, and resolve to clear out of the suburbs at once and begin to live.

Most of my books are written at the tables of such establishments, or else in cheap caffs. I cannot work in the great libraries among scholars, books and leather

ABC

BETTY walls

T.SPlatter
Exmouth Market

armchairs. The last two will often, the first always, let you down. I like to go where the floors are sanded, where the eels are greenest, where the cups of tea are thickest and sweetest, where the steam from the geyser rises to the Lincrusta ceiling, where the mirrored walls reflect an infinite progression of humble Londoners, infinitely distorted and where the world, if not my oyster, is at least my bowl of jellied eels, and all that I have on my plate is a slice of super-loaf. In such circumstances, hidden from the world behind a towering bottle of Flag sauce, these books are hammered out, word by word, between mouthfuls of mash and draughts of Tizer.

Opposite the jellied eel saloon is Redford's, a genuine old-fashioned tobaccon-

ist, complete with a period cash register, vintage adverts and tobacco jars; outside is the traditional hanging sign representing a roll of plug. It is worth while going beyond the market to Myddelton Street, a continuation. Here are interesting early nineteenth-century terraces of the best Finsbury pattern—particularly at the far end —of grey London stock brick, with well-designed Greek honeysuckle balconies at the first floor level. A number of contemporary shop fronts remain *in situ*, some still protected by the original iron bars fixed in front of the small paned windows.

If, as is likely, you discover that the shell fish or jellied eels have caused you to thirst, there is a remedy at hand: draught Guinness, a speciality of the house, at the Coach and Horses, where in addition to disposing of the thirst you can study an interesting set of paintings on mirror glass of the 1890s, the subjects being birds, butterflies and waterlilies, very possibly by a Clerkenwell-based artist, for many of these 'brilliant' mirrors were produced in the district.

Then cut through Goode Street and Sekforde Street to Clerkenwell Green, where I spend too much of my time at a marble-topped table in a café, eyeing the old men ascending and descending the lavatory steps. Things to be seen on the way include the fine Finsbury Bank for Savings of the mid-1840s—a charming piece of Pall Mall Renaissance unaccountably strayed into Finsbury—in Sekforde Street, the eighteenth-century terraced houses in Corporation Row (early Georgian with door pediments on Tuscan pilasters) and the fine houses of London brick in Sekforde Street. These date from the 1830s, and in some the Gothic glazing bars still remain in the windows. The Hugh Myddelton School on the descent down to the Green occupies the site of the Clerkenwell House of Detention, scene of the Fenian explosion in 1867 when the prison wall was blown down—or up— by gunpowder. One of the ringleaders was the last person to be publicly hanged in London. The place is worth visiting, for the house of the prison governor still remains, at an angle of the school wall.

As I have said, Clerkenwell Green is one of my favourite haunts in London. In spite of change and industrialisation, it still bears a strong impress of its rural past, with an indefinable country town air lingering about it, though the only buildings of real architectural importance—in the conventional planner's sense— are the parish church of St James, built between 1788–92 by James Carr, and the Sessions House. The church is well sited and the spire extremely fine, though the building as a whole may be described as highly competent, like the best academic art, without being inspired. A nunnery, dedicated to St Mary, once stood on the site. It was suppressed in 1539, and the buildings were gradually demolished, the last remaining portions disappearing at the end of the eighteenth century. The nunnery church itself was pulled down in 1788 to make way for the present building.

The building of the Palladian Middlesex Sessions House in 1779 must have appeared to the inhabitants of Clerkenwell as one of the several metropolitan improvements—the others being the new hospitals, the new roads, Finsbury

BANDA

Italian Church
Saffron Hill

Terroni Son
Brownsbury

Square and the new estate called Pentonville, begun in 1773—that were turning the district from a suburban to an urban area. The Sessions House was built in 1779–82 by Thomas Rogers, who drew largely on earlier designs made by John Carter in 1774. The entrance hall was altered in 1860, and the double staircase replaced by a less satisfactory design. Since 1919 the building has been occupied by various business firms and the interior arrangements much altered, though some good plaster work remains: note the Palladian front with decorative reliefs by Nollekens.

There is a plan to tidy up Clerkenwell Green: I would far rather leave it as it is, with its weary old trees, lavatory, pubs, remnants of old houses hiding behind later shop fronts and the Marx Memorial Library. None of the Marx family—neither the surrealist brothers nor the depressing Karl—has had anything to do with the place, which was once the Welsh Charity School, built in 1737 'for instructing, clothing and apprenticing indigent children born of Welsh parents, in or near London'. Clerkenwell (the well, rediscovered in 1924, can still be seen on application to the local library) was once the place where London apprentices and their girls went to sample the delights of the tea gardens of Sadler's and Bagnigge Wells. It is the London of 'Sally in our Alley'. Cardinal Manning turned up on the Green in the early 1870s during his campaign to save the souls of the poor but drunken Irish by forswearing whisky and other strong liquors, but the place settled down again, and this air of suspended animation—in fact, really peace during much of the day and especially at weekends—will I hope continue to be one of its attractions. Besides, the Green has its own fish-and-chip shop, near the steep little alley going up to the church, to delight the heart of the London fancier and to strengthen his frame for further perambulation.

Clerkenwell is the centre of the London clock-making and jewellery trades, in the same way as the area round Mortimer Street is of the rag trade and the neighbourhood of the City Road of the greeting-card firms. The district was once full of characters such as Tom Hearn, who specialised in hiring out barrows to the costermongers, his own equipage consisting of a smart dog cart with a high-stepping horse, and a Dalmation bringing up the rear between the back wheels.

Jerusalem Passage, a place of cafés and small mixed businesses (but once inhabited by jewellers and craftsmen who worked in their shop windows), leads to St John's Square, now industrialised but with one side occupied by eighteenth-century houses and an especially attractive eighteenth-century shop at the far end.

In the distance is St John's Gate, the most complete fragment above ground of the Priory of St John of Jerusalem. It is associated with Dr Johnson who worked in the room above as a literary hack long before the great Dictionary days. *The Gentleman's Magazine*, a genteel, dilettante publication, which did much to foster the taste for the picturesque, was printed at St John's Gate until 1781. (These old gateways of London were frequently put to unlikely uses; my own bank, Messrs Child and Company, whose unsatisfactory customers have included

Nell Gwynn besides myself, used to store their ledgers in Temple Bar.) Parts of the Priory church also survive, in spite of the severe damage during the last war and the rebuilding of 1958.

After passing to the Crown, the gatehouse returned to the Order in 1873. Through it you can make your way to Smithfield, by turning right at the far end, and visit the church of St Bartholomew the Great, all that is left of another great Norman and medieval priory, and see the few ancient gabled houses of Cloth Fair, rescued by my friend the late Lord Mottistone (a true lover of London) and his partner Paul Paget, the present surveyor of St Paul's.

Otherwise, retrace your route back into Clerkenwell Green and cross to the bottom part of Clerkenwell Road, making, perhaps, a slight detour (if in the early part of the day) to visit the handful of bookstalls that represent the Farringdon Market. If your luck is in, you might find the poems of Martin Tupper, a book on clinical pathology or a pamphlet on Moral Rearmament. Herbal Hill, on one side of Clerkenwell Road, and Saffron Hill, on the other, are merely fragrant names from the past; not a herb is to be seen there now, except perhaps a pot of mignonette or nasturtium on a window sill in the summer time.

The Italian church (page 22) serves, as I have said, the Italians who came here in considerable numbers in the 1880s, though the influx began before that—as far back as the 1840s, when some of the scientific men like Negretti and Zambra came to seek London's hospitality. St Peter's has a wide nave, rather splendid Ionic columns of marble and ceilings painted in a style distantly resembling that of Guido Reni. Go in, if only to see the old Italian women, with faces like withered apples, at prayer: it is pure Naples in London. In the early years of this century, the most notable event for the Italian community of Clerkenwell—Little Italy— was the festival of the Madonna dell' Carmine. Italians from all parts of London came for the festivities. Onions, plaster statuettes, ice cream and the 'art figures' the boys sold at street doors were put aside, and the dingy streets and Victorian blocks decorated with festoons, garlands, flags and holy pictures. Even the narrow courts, alleys and little houses were transformed: out came the highly coloured lithographs, the holy-water fonts and the cheap medallions of the Virgin. It was a time for gaiety and dressing up, particularly for the great religious procession that stopped the traffic. The procession is still held, though some of its vitality and picturesqueness has gone, along with the *sancta povertas*. For in those days, the colony lived in real Italian fashion, the washing women ironing and cooking outdoors, the men making hokey pokey and trundling barrows, and all but the barrel organ craftsmen and those who worked in wood, stone or mosaic were seldom far from the verge of mendicancy. One thing, however, has not changed. Though many were born here in Little Italy and will live out their lives in London, there are not many who have entirely given up hope of seeing Italy before they die. As they hand you your spaghetti, your bowl of minestrone, your bottle of Lacryma Christi, they have a far away look in their eyes.

III

Wellclose Square Revisited

———————— * ————————

WHEN I HEARD that the rag merchants who occupied Wilton's Music Hall had departed and that the place was awaiting demolition, together with the rest of Cable Street, I thought it was time to revisit Wellclose Square, while there was still one brick left standing on another. There was a time when the whole area was considered salubrious and desirable. I went down Mansell Street, one of the four streets that bounded the open space called Tenter Ground, once used for the bleaching of cloth. Of the mansions that were built there in the eighteenth century, all that remains today in Mansell Street are two three-storey merchants' houses, Nos. 57 and 59, both in a peeling and woebegone condition, both used by manufacturing firms in the rag trade. The tall, ball-topped stucco pillars remain on the street, denuded of their linking railings. No. 57 has a fine door, with a broken pediment and Roman Doric columns. Strange mildews disfigure the stucco, East End dirt eats away the brick and the relics of meths men—piles of bottles—repose in the areas. Still, in spite of their down-at-heel appearance, this pair of Georgian houses contrives to express good breeding in the manner of a penniless nobleman.

The way to Wellclose Square can take in other interesting items: the Catholic church of the English Martyrs, Gothic Revival, and a couple of eighteenth-century houses (one with a rusticated door of Coade Stone)—the remnants of a collection removed by wartime damage and clearance—in Prescot Street and St Mark Street. Stand at the door of the Scarborough Arms, and survey the typical mid-nineteenth-century artisans' dwellings in Scarborough Street—two storey in red and yellow brick, with round headed windows and doors—and take in the prefabs on the spare ground opposite, which impart a pleasingly mournful 1947 quality to the composition. Opposite the Scarborough Arms are three-storey blocks of grey stock brick, with flat and shallow arched windows and severe pilastered doors, proving how the Georgian tradition persisted in the East London of the mid-Victorian age. The rest of the route takes in the lower part of Leman Street, with the C.W.S. Bank (1930 Dutch style) at the corner, Cable Street and Grace's Alley, haunted by poor immigrants and Casey Court kids.

The devastation in the square was pitiful to see. I only saw one man all the time I paced the square, and he had one foot in the grave. The April evening was chill and the sky overcast, but a blackbird warbled in the plane trees, introducing impromptu variations and evidently trying to keep his courage up. The half dozen Georgian terraced houses left on the North side looked indescribably weary and exhausted, their bricks crumbling and their stucco returning to sand. Grass was coming up on the pavement. One house was still occupied and displayed a few geraniums flowering bravely between lace curtains of a Great Exhibition pattern. On the East side, the small early nineteenth-century warehouse (the harbinger of the square's decline) which I had always intended to draw had also gone. As I walked round, the blackbird resumed his song, after a pause during which, like many Cable Street people, he had been to fetch his supper.

The best part of the square in recent years was the group of old houses on the South—between the corner of the square and the Courthouse. These were still there, but boarded up with their own dismantled shutters.

When I returned to the alley, I made the drawing reproduced opposite. Wilton's has an interesting history. Moreover, it is notable architecturally, for the severity of its interior is relieved only by the fibrous plaster work of the single gallery and the barley-sugar columns that support it; the decorative motifs of this plasterwork—swags, roses, sunflowers and the like—are repeated in the extremely well modelled pilaster strips on the door jambs, the whole being another example of the persistence of the refined taste of the Georgians carried over into a later period. In the 1830s, the site of Wilton's was occupied by a pub, The Prince of Denmark, known to sailormen and the press gangs as The Mahogany Bar. John Wilton took it over in 1850 and introduced music-hall type entertainment with such success that his own music-hall followed, the foundation stone being laid by his wife, Ellen, in 1858. Sam Collins, later to open Collins's on Islington Green, was on the opening bill in 1859. Wilton's, famous not only for its stars but also for its stupendous cut-glass chandelier, closed in 1880, reopening eventually as a mission and soup kitchen—a characteristic East End destiny fulfilled—until finally the rags moved in.

The blackbird was still presenting his own musical entertainment and, as I finished the drawing, two young women came down the alley. Glancing up, they saw the notice on the door.

'Wilton's Music Hall,' says the first, 'whatever in the world's that?'

'Why,' replies her friend, 'don'tcher know? It's that corny old-time stuff you see on the telly, where they're all wearin' old clo'.'

Where they're all wearing old clo'! It was time, high time, I felt, to take leave of Wellclose Square, once a genteel residence for Danish and Norwegian merchants, and now a lot of old rubble. So I did, by way of Leman Street. But there was one surprise in store. Half-way down is the last of the Georgian mansions in that gloomy thoroughfare. It has been many things in its time, including a doss-house, and for years past just an empty shell, a haunt for derelicts and cast-offs, human, animal, vegetable and mineral. I had considered it beyond the power of

26

anyone to restore, even supposing anyone were willing. Somebody *was* restoring it, however; a prime example of putting new wine in old bottles. The old faded announcement on the wall, 'The Manor House—good beds for working men,' had been obliterated. The working men themselves, that seem to have been left over from Morris and the mid-century philanthropists, are also being obliterated: the reformers did their work too well. Soon we shall have to keep the doss-houses going artificially—like the stately homes—at half-a-crown a head.

Indian shops — Drummond St., Euston

IV

Sidewalks of Camden

———— ✳ ————

A DWELLER IN A NEAT SEMI (christened after his wife's name spelt backwards) in the suburbs, who washes his car, cuts the lawn at weekends, does as he is bidden, acts reasonably and pays his taxes, can only be considered happy if he has not, as most of us have, a Bohemian inside him, striving to get out. How many respectable suburban men would like to kick over the traces and disappear like Mr Polly; would like to take up with a loose woman and live free and easy in squalid surroundings in a place such as Camden? Lots, I hope. Camden Town is ideal for this, for the architectural background is agreeable, and the people racially and socially mixed, and they mind their own business. I have been haunting it for years, with daily increasing zest.

The place is a work of art in itself; the pavements constitute a grey canvas on which London paints an endless succession of pictures of low life, changing them on the instant to something fresh, but always in a minor key. Instead of studying at the Slade, I spent most of my days wandering its streets and my evenings in cheap cafés or at the Bedford. But, of course, like everywhere else, it is being ruined by rebuilding. It is coming up in the world, in the intellectual planner's estimation, having been down since the coming of the railways. Nonetheless, in street after street you can still relish the cat-haunted areas—where they kept the pig-bins in my student days—admire old men sleeping in the sun in little asphalted parks and gaze up at the cracked stucco of house fronts, where yellow faces still peer from behind lace curtains.

When the film was made from my book *The London Nobody Knows*, I imagined that the shots I had planned might be difficult after all, but the streets were full of grey-lined heads, all peering through curtains and between sickly plants, and anxious to be photographed, so strengthening my belief that Nature imitates Art.

I like to begin a session in the area from a point in the region of Euston, such as Drummond Street. When I first knew it, Drummond Street was one of the ordinary small working-class streets north of Euston, with a toyshop that hung its toy horses outside and a couple of ancient electric lamps bending from the fascia. There was an old-fashioned dairy—it is still there, fortunately—with jugs of flowers in the window in the summer time.

Today there are more Indians in the street than Londoners, and most of the old shops are occupied by Indian restaurants, Indian and Pakistani butchers, poulterers, grocers and confectioners. I like to go to Patak's (opposite) where, in addition to a bewildering assortment of spices, curries and sugar candy, are fresh vegetables flown in from India. Indian sweetmeats, ruinous to the figure but otherwise eminently desirable, are a speciality. These include Rose Halwa, flavoured with roses, and Almond Halwa, and there are two kinds of Barfi—the delicious green made out of pistachio nuts and the plain yellow. There is also the triangular vegetable savoury, Samosa, rather like a Cornish pasty, a couple of which with a mug of tea form the Indian working-man's dinner. Altogether the street has become an Indian suburb.

Gower Street, at the Hampstead Road end, is still unspoiled: there are still the time-honoured area dustbins, the yellow-grey lace curtains, the faded paintwork of the railings and the general air of exhaustion and decay. Here and there a few pots of ivy keep up a losing battle for existence on the sills or on the damp paving of the area. One or two small hotels (h and c in all rooms) keep up a gallant fight against hateful change and the spread of flyovers, underpasses and office and university blocks, and there is still a sprinkling of cafés and barbers' shops. But for the true decay, the run down hopelessness and nightmare flavour turn into Tolmer's Square (pages 32/33). There is nowhere quite like it in other parts of London. It ought to be preserved, with its inhabitants, just as it stands, a mute protest against technocrats and progress. The square, actually two mutilated segments of an oval open at each end, is unbelievably decayed and crumbling to ruin. Some of the houses appear never to have been painted since they were built, and the porticos thereof have lost heart entirely. It has been too much lived in, Tolmer's Square. Cast iron, barley sugar lamp standards lean this way and that, and there are a few Regency bollards marked with the monogram of George IV.

As you wander, grey faces appear and disappear at the windows of the four-storied houses, and an old woman in black comes out to throw a stale loaf to the innumerable pigeons waiting on the crazy granite setts; not that they need feeding, for the pavements abound with superannuated fragments of food, including chips, cake and remnants of kippers. As the door opens, you have a glimpse of a dark, greasy hall, and the pent up smells of a century or so of cooking, subtly mingled with those of the domestic cat, make their escape. In the centre is the Tolmer cinema, once a church (the Gothic buttresses covered with cement rendering remain on the sides), towards which the old age pensioners are hobbling—dark black beetle-like figures, old couples most of them, that give you the feeling they are going into the Ark. A kid kicks an empty box, and knocks over a pile of milk bottles, and bottles left by vinos. An old man who has decided against embarkation stares at a faded poster which reads 'Jeger for St Pancras'.

You can visit the square again and again, and each time find it hard to believe you are not having an uneasy dream. Tolmer's Square is perfect for a film of desolation—one that would build up by means of close shots of tired eyes, irresolute feet and London rubbish that emptiness, dislocation and sense of not belonging which is so characteristic of these areas—but most backers would go to earth at the thought of it, and most distributors would take to the hills.

The best way to Camden is to walk along Hampstead Road, savouring the last remnants of the original terraces, with shops built out from the original façades in typical London fashion, and seeing the well-proportioned, crumbling, terraced streets such as Netley Street and Robert Street, all made to look unnecessarily tatty and despairing by the Post Office Tower which dominates them and has its eye on them, knowing them to be written off, and by the new blocks of flats closing in on all sides, especially in the direction of Camden Town. Sickert worked in this quarter, and latter-day variants of the mouldy, inconclusive and evasive bed-sitting subjects by which he established a new genre can still be found here, at least for the moment.

The Prince of Wales pub and, at the other side of the passage, Walter Davies's, the pawnbroker's, are of the genuine old time. Next to the pub was J. Bryce-Smith's, an old-established but somewhat eccentric artists' colourman's. Their shop is now a 'turf accountant's', but the wall above still displays their name. Bryce-Smith's was called 'the artist's graveyard' from their practice—unusual but helpful—of trading in the tools and materials of deceased artists. Sometimes one could pick up rare bargains there—fine oil colours by firms long defunct, brushes of Edwardian or Victorian vintage, when such things were made to last. Near by is Nicholson's, 'late Britain', with a mid-nineteenth-century front, a period pharmacy which has been closed for donkey's years—at any rate, I have never seen it open— and there is the dust of ages over the faded display cards, patent medicines and carboys. It is a typical chemist's shop of its time, rather refined and dignified; the fascia has black lettering on a gold ground.

On the left side of Hampstead Road as you approach Mornington Crescent is the once dignified, though somewhat heavy, stuccoed terrace associated with Dickens and his illustrator, the gifted and still undervalued George Cruikshank. Cruickshank's house, marked with a plaque, is at the far end, nearest to Camden High Street; the house, though recently repainted, is now very mournful, and like the rest of the terrace, divided off into rooms; a few stunted trees carry on an unequal struggle for existence in the soured front gardens. Dickens, at the opposite end, has fared even worse, for the house occupied by the private school he attended has gone altogether, but you can still trace out how the school playground was truncated by the coming of the railway, as the novelist mentions in his essay.

Camden High Street is guarded, as it were, by a mediocre statue of Cobden, father of Sickert's first wife. There used to be a gents' lavatory of remarkable quality at this point, rich with metalwork and tile. I used to frequent the Cobden island, not only for the lavatory, but also for the Victorian coffee stall. At its counter gathered a regular army of lonely old men from bed-sits and those yet lonelier ones who lived with in-laws who didn't want them. They used to exchange reminiscences of Camden in the old times, of stars like Wilkie Bard and Marie Lloyd in their heyday at the Bedford, and would argue for hours on the respective merits of bottled coffee, whether Camp or Distil or Bev was the best; each brand had its advocates; and so argued the drinkers of meat extract; some were for Bovril, others declared for Oxo; Marmite had its adherents, who swore there was nothing to touch it, and the merits and warming capacity of Betox were fully canvassed.

I used to have an early supper at the Bedford Café, off egg and chips or Vienna steak, with generous dollops of Flag Sauce, spend the evening at the Bedford and finish the night at the coffee stall before walking back to my parlour in the sky in Bloomsbury. It was a good life, and it was a good club—the coffee stall club— though the old men repeated themselves a good deal, physically and verbally. But it had the strange no-flavour I relish so much. Unlike most clubs, which are auto-cratic and selective, it was run on democratic lines. There was a complete absence of formality which appealed to me. Besides, there were no fees once you had paid for your pie and cuppa, and there was always the fun of guessing which of several

MON·MARCH 6TH
3 DAYS
EDWARD G·ROBINSON
JOAN BLONDELL

CINCINATTI
KID

famous hotels, at home and abroad, or which of the world's railway systems would provide you with your crockery that night.

Cobden stands opposite the Camden Theatre, meditating Corn Law politics and eyeing the Camden-towners as they emerge from the Tube, returning to bed-sitters in the peeling terraces of the district. Sometimes a Greek funeral passes, a line of cars smothered in 'floral tributes'. Here is the world's most famous second-hand clothes shop, much esteemed and patronised by the members of the theatrical profession. One of them beat me to a rich and splendid fur coat, opulent and Oscar Wilde-like, of a kind I have always coveted, in this establishment only recently, and refused to resell it to me, though I pleaded my need was greater than his and that the label, of a famous Savile Row tailor, demanded an owner out of the ordinary.

Higher up, on the opposite side, is the shell of the Old Bedford, condemned to demolition and classed as a dangerous structure. One of the many paintings Sickert did of the interior is in the Tate Gallery. Until recently the place was a nightly refuge for tramps and junkies. For the moment, the Bedford, plastered over with posters, appears as a melancholy symbol of the extinction of that once popular London entertainment, the music hall. Behind the building, its pub, the Bedford Arms, still flourishes—one of Camden's Irish pubs—the others being the Camden Stores and the Brighton.

Opposite the Bedford is Pratt Street, part of Camden's Greek and Cypriot colony. At this point, if you are weary of wandering like Xenophon's army, you can sample at an incredibly modest price some of the delicious Greek dishes at one of the little restaurants. You can take your time—for the Greeks are in no hurry—over Turkish coffee; you can read a Greek newspaper, if you have a mind to, or muse over the classic ruins of Camden, the Bedford among them. My regular Greek café is the Paphos: all the customers speak Greek, all know each other and the proprietors, all are immensely good humoured, all smoke incessantly and play games of chance.

Half-way down Pratt Street is the St Martin's Tavern. By its side is the entrance to the churchyard garden of St Martin's. There are a few Gothic and classic tombs distributed about the lawns and flower beds; one of the tombs is that of Charles Dibden, the composer of nautical ballads. It is a place where old men meditate among the iris and rambler roses, where cats take their morning promenade. When the air raid shelters were being dug in the early days of the war, the excavators found so many human remains of the bodies buried there during the Plague that the work was abandoned; the mound in the centre of the garden marks the position of the burial pit.

The Greek community has its own church, All Saints, by the Inwoods, suitably in the Greek Revival style. It may be compared with the same architects' costlier and more showy church of St Pancras, Woburn Place, one of the earliest neo-Grecian churches in London and in its exterior elevations incorporating features borrowed wholesale from the Erechtheum and the Tower of the Winds, and round the corner in Woburn Walk, the delightful stucco Grecian style shops, often ascribed to Cubitt, who, however, only built them: they, like the two churches mentioned, are by the Inwoods. All Saints has a semicircular portico with four great Ionic columns; Ionic columns also support the gallery in the interior, where the work of the architect blends admirably with the icons and candles of the Greek Orthodox Church.

But the great attraction in this part of Camden is the street market held in Inverness Street, just beyond the Camden Town tube station (below). Fruit, flowers and vegetables sold from brilliantly lit stalls are its main concern, but at the top end are a number of stalls offering a plentiful supply of junk. There are cruets enough to furnish all the apartment houses in Bloomsbury, tar inhalers made by Boots at a remote period ('Two shillings, skipper,' said the vendor, 'there's nothing

like a Boots inhaler when your nose is stuffed up.'), bird cages, books, violins, art nouveau figurines with their arms broken, boxes of records (Primo Scala's Accordeon Band, Vera Lynn's 'White Cliffs of Dover' and the Celest Octet are the first handful; these I reverently return for music hall is what I am after; presently I come up with an early Sandy Powell) and innumerable other frowsy objects. Among these, on one of my visits, was a Victorian dentist's chair in red plush, with a cut glass spitoon and ornamental ironwork below—a survivor of the early days when anyone with a wrist strong enough and a front parlour could set up in business.

Other survivors are the antique television and wireless sets. Some of these scratched and battered TVs are only a few years old, yet they appear to have come out of the Ark. You wonder why you allowed such ugly mugs, such malevolent brutes, in your household, and feel that, though the heroes of a thousand quizzes, they fully deserve to be marked down at ten bob. The wireless sets belong to the age of Jack Payne and Amy Johnson; you seem to hear "Daventry calling . . . Daventry calling' crackling out of the sun-ray fronts. Others with greasy decoration in bakelite belong to the 1930s. If only we could tune in once more and listen to Henry Hall with the B.B.C. Dance Orchestra and Val Rosing! Such considerations depress me on the instant, for I have always been afraid of Time and what it does to us, and my spirits are not uplifted by seeing an old dame buy an old faded lithograph, Alma-Tadema-like and very fusty, called 'Whispers of Love'. I begin to wish I had bought the tar inhaler to clear my head.

Therefore, I turn to another favourite port of call, the Greek Food centre, noting a new collector's item on the pavement—a machine for selling paraffin, a mechanical Esso-blue dealer. Almost everything that Greece exports in foods, wines and fresh vegetables can be bought at this shop, and the proprietors are more than willing to give Greek recipes to customers. The vegetables from Greece or Cyprus include coriander, Greek parsley and okra. You can buy fresh pastries, including those made with Greek honey from Mount Hymettus, and a wide selection of bread. Wines from Crete, Corfu, Cyprus and the Greek mainland are a speciality. Each Greek wine comes from a particular area. From Crete comes the red wine, Archanai, and there is the white dry wine from the region of Chalkis. The most select wine from Corfu is Mont Kerkis. Retsina, which has a resin added, is a curiously flavoured wine, admirable for summer drinking. This is, perhaps, the Greek wine best known in this country. Probably the finest of all is the red sweet wine from the Peloponnese. This, known as Mavrodaphne, is reputed to be the wine Homer drank, and is used as an aperitif. The customers are almost as interesting as the foodstuffs, and by the time I come out, loaded with bread, wine and honey, I have forgotten all about Val Rosing and the years that have gone with the wind.

Inverness Street, Arlington Road and a few streets in the area have a number of early and very interesting electric light standards (page 37). There is a flavour of

SP Patchin
Arlington Road
Camden Town

William Morris about the flower and leaf decoration, but the most remarkable feature about these lamps is the figure of the boy-martyr, St Pancras, complete with aureole, contained in a Greek-style framework. These show how far we have travelled from the turn of the century: what local authority, even if it had a patronal saint, would today consider putting his effigy and superscription on a lamp standard? The lamps at the west end of the Strand, with the beautifully designed medallion of St Martin dividing his cloak with the beggar, belong to the same genre; like those of St Pancras, they are distinctly old-hat.

Parkway is a line of communication between the side-walks of Camden and the refined regions of the Park. It contains one of London's most famous pet shops, where parrots peer knowlingly at you and where delightful period-type birdcages can be bought, and Roberson's, the artists' colourmen, who made colours for Millais, the Pre-Raphaelites and many of the notable watercolour painters of the early nineteenth century. They have one of Millais's palettes, presented to the firm by Lady Millais, and one of the brushes bound in twine which Roberson's made especially for him.

At the top of Parkway is Park Village, laid out by Nash and his assistant, Sir James Pennethorne, from 1824 onwards as a flourish to terminate the great Regents Park scheme. The villas, in a variety of Italian, Classic and Gothic styles, imitated later in the pattern books of Loudon and Robinson, were designed to be a picturesque offset to the formality of the terraces by the Park. Park Village East consists of a number of villas in a line, set among trees and ivy grown gardens; Park Village West is grouped round a little winding street. A spring evening is the best time to see Park Village—when there are blue violet shadows in the chestnuts and planes, and the lilac and the last of the yellow jasmine is out in the gardens.

A lot of rich Victorian ironwork is found here—a bas-relief of the martyrdom of St Pancras set in the parapet of the bridge, ornate lamp standards and one of my favourite London drinking fountains, with a figure of a girl perched on a pile of rocks: the rocks are only stone-faced; behind that craggy pile are courses of brickwork. All this metalwork and sculpture is in the style of the Great Exhibition,

Albany Street is the main thoroughfare of a secondary group by Nash, consisting of a market, shopping streets and artisans' houses. Not much of his scheme is left today; modern blocks of flats and modern pubs have altered the streets almost beyond recognition, but one or two terraces, Christ Church and a Regency pub, the Prince George of Cumberland, aid in jogging the memory. Pennethorne was the architect of Christ Church, which was opened in 1837. There are massive cornices, round headed windows and great doors, with finely designed consoles and mouldings, on the pattern of the Erechtheum, and a somewhat reedy tower and spire which from most angles appears too slight for the massive bulk of the church.

The entire design is a perfect example of what Pugin castigated as 'Pagan' in his books of architectural polemics, on the assumption that the word was a valid term of criticism. Of course, it was not; nevertheless there are certain neo-greek churches, of which Christ Church is one, in which an implicit pessimism is present —a lack of reassurance that even the most professional architectural critic (one concerned purely with formal considerations) might consider as uncomfortably at variance with the purposes of the building. The design is austere to the point of severity. It is almost successful for the same reason that contemporary American Greek was successful—simplicity in arrangement is combined with a use of Greek forms towards an individual purpose, as opposed to mere academic borrowing or an assembling of ready made ingredients. But, as I have said, the mass of the church is too ponderous for the spire, the cornice is heavy and clumsy, the grey stock brick —not the most attractive material for the purpose—has become discoloured and the artificial stone has weathered badly. The best view of it is from the corner of Redhill Street. Christ Church contains a rarity that alone makes a pilgrimage rewarding—a stained glass window by Rossetti.

Only the pink and grey granite setts, a water conduit and some iron bollards with the monogram of George IV remain from the famous Cumberland Market, once a huge open space where the hay-carts deposited their loads, surrounded by small, unpretending Regency houses which gave it the look of the main square of some half-baked French provincial town. On sunny afternoons the whole place went to sleep, including the horses themselves, dozing over their nosebags. Huge blocks of flats, bewildering to anyone who remembers the old streets and corner pubs, now occupy the site; horses, loads of hay and houses have been blown away like a straw from the market, and the new generations amusing themselves in the council's melancholy play-area and sandpit know them not.

But the market had its recording angels in the shape of Sickert and Robert Bevan, the latter actually basing himself for a period at 49 Cumberland Market, where he formed a group named after it. His paintings and drawings of the area rank with those of the meagre uplands round Swiss Cottage as among his most distinctive work.

Wind up by going through the market, between the giant blocks, to Stanhope Street, where a few worn out old houses remain with delicate balconies, a fragment of what was once perhaps the most interesting part of Camden, peopled almost entirely, as I used to think, by old women in black, men dozing at pub corners in anticipation of opening time, street traders and horses. I wish I had had the sense to record it before it vanished. All I can do now is to stand among the towering blocks, meditate over change and progress and listen to the chimes of the ice cream man, Mister Softee, who adds his melody to the April evening.

Spring Evening
Islington Green
G S Fletcher

V

'Thy Fields, Fair Islington!'

———— * ————

Thy fields, fair Islington! begin to bear
Unwelcome buildings, and unseemly piles;
The streets are spreading, and the Lord knows where
Improvement's hand will spare the neighb'ring stiles . . .

THE ABOVE, part of a poem from William Hone's *Table Book*, is as true now—or
at least the second line of it—as when it was written in 1827. 'Unwelcome buildings
and unseemly piles' are, for that matter, a feature generally applicable to London,
but Islington, up to now a perfectly unspoiled working-class area with a distinctive

architectural character imparted by fine, if neglected, eighteenth-century terraces and such splendid later developments as the villas of Northampton Park and other parts of Canonbury, perfect for authors, artists and film makers, is now being rudely shaken from its inanition.

The rebuilding of the Packington Estate—a most interesting complex of squares and terraced streets, well-proportioned though built at the very end of the Georgian tradition (the late 1840s)—can be taken as a sample of what will follow. In the end, the admittedly defective housing standards encountered in Islington will have been corrected, but the area will have had its character and life taken away and be no longer worth living in anyway.

Rebuilding was not always a certain loss. In the eighteenth century, a borough might knock its ancient church down and rebuild it in a different but entirely acceptable style: a town like Poole might be destroyed only to raise itself up again, more delightfully than before, for there were still architects then, and they were artists first and builders afterwards. Nor was it the pre-industrial conditions that fostered this, for the great early nineteenth-century engineers like Brunel were not only constructionists, but they were also endowed with the capacity to create their own architectural style, at once authentic and austere. Architects today are merely businessmen, organisers of space for human ants on whom penal laws and the tyranny of bureaucrats have been and are being exercised to a degree truly shameful.

What with this and the proliferation of the motor-car and roads to run the accursed things on, the outlook for London as a place to enjoy life at the end of the century is highly unpromising. It is on the cards that London and other cities formerly of great interest will be living hells. By the time the process reaches its appointed end, the simpletons who so confidingly accepted the systems they grew up under—the boss men, technocrats and planners they allowed, with decreasing concern and feebler resistance, to get the upper hand—may realise at last that they (the complacent English) have been sold down the river in the original meaning of the expression. Then there may be a reaction. If so, we may yet be treated to the spectacle of some scientist being forced to experiment on himself, some bureaucrat having his mouth stuffed with his own demolition order and some planner, head first down a lavatory, being flushed out of the street his masters were proposing—of course in the interests of the public—to rebuild. But I very much doubt it. My own belief is that everything that made life worth living in cities like London, Manchester, Birmingham and the unique industrial towns of the North, like Oldham, will be utterly destroyed.

Whenever I am low in spirits or whenever I feel I have deserved particularly well of myself, I take myself off for a half day or so to Islington. It is the cheapest entertainment in London and one of the best. I invariably begin on the Green, where the statue of Myddelton rises from the ironwork of the women's lavatory (page 40). (Incidentally, the men's lavatory nearer the Angel, opposite the shell of the Grand, is an interesting early specimen by Doultons: their William Morris style nameplate in tile can be seen on the way down, and there has been little or no modernisation inside.) I spend a long time gazing at the art nouveau undertaker's on the Green—'Please ask for Memorial Catalogue'; then I go for a meal in a snack bar and work in a visit to the amusement arcade to join the youths and mournful women at the one-armed-bandits. All this is just an appetiser; from now on I am in a mood to select from a wide range of possibilities.

Islington begins at the Angel. Ease of access and the quality of the squares and terraces, built from the beginning of the eighteenth century to about 1850, have as much to do with its popularity as cheapness had until recently. The original Angel, with a galleried yard used for dramatic performances, was demolished in 1819. The inn that followed was rebuilt in 1880, and turned into a massive Victorian pub: the old-fashioned wainscoted parlours filled with cattlemen and country cousins went out, and in came plate glass and splendid bars. Lyons's Angel Café (now closed)—a fin de siècle building of much interest—more or less occupies the site. You can go past the derelict Grand, already mentioned, a Victorian classic façade plastered over with advertisements, and along the Camden Passage. Antique shops line the alley, and there is a market for antiques consisting of open-air stalls held on Saturday.

Camden Passage has changed out of all recognition in recent years. Lock-up antique shops, called Montpelier Row, occupy the site of the little old dirty cottages (called Paradise Row or Paradise Place, I forget which) which were inhabited chiefly by poverty-stricken Irish. A fashionable restaurant occupies the corner where a toy-shop used to be (not *the* toy-shop—the dolls' hospital—which was farther along beyond the Camden Head), and a general air of prosperity has replaced the old feeling of going down the drain. But Lou's secondhand clothes shop remains triumphantly itself, and so does the gramophone shop and the sewing machine shop next to it: there are few artifacts I like more than old sewing machines. All the old right-angled lamps have gone too—wickedly replaced by concrete poles.

Half way down is Charlton Place, run down and full of sloppy women when I first knew it, but now breaking out into blue and olive-green doors, white Venetian blinds and backyards transmogrified into patios. Backyards are out; no one will own up to having one: Northern accents were at a similar discount until Harold Wilson brought them back into favour.

Charlton Place leads to Duncan Terrace, where you will find some of the finest Georgian houses in Islington. Until recently there was a notice board in a yard near Elia Street (Elia Street after Charles Lamb, whose cottage, no longer pleasantly rural, survives in Colebrooke Row, a continuation of Duncan Terrace) which offered 'Sedan Chairs for Hire. Chairs for Balls, Routs and Assemblies'. Also in Colebrooke Row, almost opposite to Lamb's cottage, you can still read a vintage announcement which has come to light as the layers of superimposed paint peel off the wall:

Hotel for Women only. 9d. per night
6/- per week.

The letters, about a foot high, could no doubt be easily read from Essex Road.

The coming to light of old wall signs is an interesting study: I have been a collector of painted, submerged walls for years. Ordinary mural decorations usually bore me, but I am excessively fond of forgotten adverts on gable ends. There is one in Clapham, advertising an Electric Theatre. I have an early Gillette one in my collection, a furniture repository one in Vauxhall, a number of tobacco and condensed milk announcements. These and amateur graffiti are among the true pleasures of urban life. Two of my recent acquisitions in the second category are rare and choice: 'Keep Billy Graham off the Moon' and, in the Whitechapel area, a truly period one, a magnificent survival full of nostalgia from the Vera Lynn period, 'Open the Second Front Now'.

I have already mentioned the Rex on Islington Green (page 14), but not the remains of the old chapel, a cut-price Greek façade, at the side of the cinema in Providence Place. A few yards farther along Upper Street and also worth seeing is the 1880-style, cut brick and sandstone depot of 'The London Salvage Corps': the big double doors the horses once galloped through are still intact.

Off Duncan Terrace is Vincent Terrace. Between it and the backs of the houses in Noel Road is the Regent's Canal. Sickert painted and etched the subject on several occasions and the title he gave to one of the paintings, 'The Hanging Gardens of Islington', although unofficial, has stuck to the place. The rear portions of the houses have pointed windows and crenellated parapets—features (page 45) that obviously prompted Sickert to call another painting of the subject 'Fading Memories of Sir Walter Scott', an allusion at once erudite and amusing. These houses are now coming up in the world, in common with other parts of Islington, and are painted in pale blues, pinks, lilacs and creams.

In the gardens above the canal, cast iron seats and urns are taking the place of washing as a means of decoration, but Sickert's subjects can be easily recognised. Sickert loved the sleazy blend of good proportions and faded stucco commemorated in such paintings as 'The Hanging Gardens'. In fact, he lived there himself for a time, in 1925, at 56 Noel Street (now Noel Road), a house still in existence. Also still in existence is his more famous studio, No. 1 Highbury Place, where he held one of his short-lived schools of painting, illustration and engraving.

I have recently done a good deal of research on Sickert's Islington homes and subjects, drawing largely on the knowledge and enthusiasm of the present Borough Librarian, Mr C. A. Elliott, who told me that a cab driver he once knew often had Sickert as a passenger, and that the cabby said it was not unusual for Sickert to drive around for hours looking for subjects, only to discover he had no money on him to pay the fare; not that the cab drivers ever minded for Sickert was well known and his credit good. A better known anecdote—one that Sickert himself was fond of retailing—belongs to the 1880s, when Sickert, dressed in a loud check coat and carrying a small bag, was strolling home from Hoxton and some girls in Copenhagen Street mistook him for Jack the Ripper.

Many of Sickert's Islington subjects are now much harder to identify than the Hanging Gardens, being as confusing, sometimes, as his many changes of address, but I had one piece of good fortune. This concerns the oil painting called 'Barnsbury' in the Glasgow Art Gallery. The subject is an oil and colourman's shop, Thorne & Co., a firm who had several shops in the area up to the Great War. I was put off the scent at first by the fact that the undated painting was only exhibited in 1931; it turned out to have been painted from a much earlier drawing, a frequent practice with the artist. Eventually, by a process of elimination based on the use of old directories, I found the shop, only to find the alleyway on the corner gone, and the shop, now an estate agent's, altered beyond belief. I could hardly accept it as the same, but the proof—and this is the interesting point—was in the oil jars above the fascia in the painting. These are a characteristic sign still found in London on the old oil shops—a kind of Ali-Baba jar to indicate the kind of business carried on. Thorne & Co. had gone out of business and left the premises years ago. The jars had also disappeared, but the place they once occupied still shows as an area of cleaner brick; an elementary deduction worthy, if not of Holmes, at least of Sexton Blake, and clinching the matter satisfactorily.

Sickert's Islington, as far as it can be studied today, includes the former Caledonian Market (until the site is built over) between North Road and Market Road; Duncan Terrace; Highbury Place; the Canal; and Barnsbury. I suggest its exploration as an interesting London experience—one to be undertaken before all the flavour has gone. Barnsbury, in particular, is very rich in crumbling terraces, undertakers and small mixed businesses. It is slowly coming back into favour. The area was once countrified with a popular tea garden, White Conduit House, on a site now occupied by a Victorian pub of the same name.

Barnsbury Square is worth seeing, and so is Richmond Avenue, an Egyptian curiosity which has terraced houses equipped with sphinxes and obelisks, somewhat run down and very forbidding. Barnsbury, like the rest of Islington, is evolving a new and mixed society. Artists, journalists, television producers and actors, together with the coloured population, have become as much a part of the scene as the original North London inhabitants.

One of my favourite perambulations is down Essex Road, savouring it all slowly, as far as Balls Pond. Fragments of Victorian working-class life still make themselves felt against the Welfare state background: there was a shop nearby where coal was sold in ha'porths and penn'orths until recently (as well as dealing in secondhand corsets), and sometimes on winter evenings when the kids are hanging about in front of St Peter's Church (by Barry, 1835) you feel yourself back

in the days when the boots given to the children of the district had to have the words 'NOT TO BE PAWNED' branded into the insides with a red hot knitting needle.

Fragments of the eighteenth century remain also—for example, the delightful three-sided eighteenth-century house of dark stock brick, with red dressed quoins and a 'Chinese' string course moulding, above the Home and Colonial Stores, and the fine terraces, albeit decayed, of the eighteenth century opposite, at right-

angles to Essex Road. Mixed up with all this, in fact in shops below old terraces, are serve-yourself grocers, betting offices, the do-it-yourself shops beloved of Welfare-Staters, laundrettes, florists where they prepare superbly period wreaths and floral tributes, and pawnbrokers, who still sell gold-plated Alberts for watches —new ones I mean, of course—and Victorian-type E.P.N.S. rattles with bone teething rings.

The Egyptian cinema is here, and, seeing it for the umpteenth time, I wonder if, like the Black Cat factory, the motif was the result of a fashion craze following on the discovery of Tutankhamen's tomb. Adjoining it is one of my favourite London walls—a gable end of a derelict terrace—covered over with posters (opposite). I often go up to look at the posters, to see what is new. One of the agreeable features of the so-called swinging London is the spawning of brightly coloured posters for obscure jazz groups—the best sites for them are in the neighbourhood of Lisle Street. Many of these posters are at the moment in a corrupt version of art nouveau, sometimes so bad that they cannot be read, but they are a change from the boxing and greyhound posters I have had to depend on. Besides, the names of the groups—'The Hooligans', 'The Werewolves', 'The Egg Heads' and so on—amuse me. I rate the best of these posters as highly as those for the free lectures on stammering, though the finest vintage poster in London—that for Chlorodyne—is unrivalled for period quality.

Beyond this is a fine Bloomsbury-like crescent, with a group of three houses at each corner, emphasising with their delicate cartwheel balconies the ends of the terrace on either hand (the houses in the curved sections of the crescent having only plain balconies—a subtle refinement characteristic of the Regency). Farther still is Jay's, a splendid jeweller's and pawnbroker's of truly Victorian richness, complete with projecting bracket clock, solid lettered signs and Victorian lettering in gold on the fascia: round the corner in Ockendon Road are the two doors, one marked 'Private Office for Loans' and the other simply 'Loan Office', in white porcelain letters on the fanlight, and these are the doors you enter when Uncle is really a friend in need.

But Islington, like St Pancras Station and St Paul's, is something that has to be seen for oneself: in fact it is a total experience, requiring all the senses and all the faculties. The old Islington, that is. The new one I prefer not to dwell on. Much the same thing applies to the canal systems of Camden Town and Islington, now almost entirely disused and in a state of pictorial neglect. There are those who would reactivate them, build artists' studios, marinas and coffee bars on the banks and workshops for do-it-yourself boating enthusiasts. Such schemes are characteristic of a certain kind of confused thinking all too prevalent nowadays. No such preservational change of use is necessary to get the best out of these North London canals: all that is needful is to leave them alone. They have been allowed to run down; let them remain so, in weed grown solitude and picturesque decline, for that character constitutes their chief attraction.

VI

Covent Garden and the Dials

———— ✳ ————

WHEN THE SUPREME VANDALISM of demolishing the market takes place—of course because it is not completely efficient, and efficiency is the alpha and omega of existence—this part of London, now one of the most rewarding, will become utterly barren and uninteresting—as uninteresting and uninviting as the South

Bank between the Festival Hall and County Hall, with both horrors included. Of course, we are only copying the French in their removal of Les Halles to that dumping ground in the fields between Paris and Orly, and the same loss of vitality and interest will result.

A man must be in very low water if a turn or two in the Garden cannot lighten his mind, for the objects to divert his thoughts are many and varied and served up fresh every day. Even on the hottest noon at midsummer, a current of air finds its way round the streets. That and the hosing down of the pavement and the scent of flowers and vegetables makes it an ideal place to take the air in London: it is better than the parks, for there is more going on, and I cannot but feel the superiority of a meal at one of the market pubs or at the coffee stall to the refreshment pavilions in the official open spaces.

The churchyard of St Paul's is ideal for meditation. Here are green lawns, some old trees where the sparrows cheep, comfortable, drowsy-looking Victorian benches lining the path, eight of London's finest gas lamps—Gothic lanterns on classic columns—and an old, octagonal, porters' hut.

Then there is the peace and beauty of the church itself, which was designed, as is well-known, by Inigo Jones for the Earl of Bedford in 1633. The Duke stipulated a barn of a place—that was all; but Jones built what he truthfully described as 'the Handsomest Barn in England'. Besides its architectural qualities, St Paul's is interesting from the number of remarkable people buried there, including Ellen Terry, Sir Peter Lely, Thomas Girtin and Grinling Gibbons and his wife, Elizabeth. The memorials include those to the parents of J. M. W. Turner (Turner was christened in the church), C. B. Cochran, Leslie Henson and Ivor Novello.

The Tuscan Portico at the east end was the setting for the opening sequences of the film of *Pygmalion*, and it was here that that supreme individualist, Mr Punch, made his first public appearance in England in May 1662, his debut being witnessed by Samuel Pepys. The portico is, in fact, one of the best open-air entertainments in town. You could spend a whole day there—I have in fact done so several times —without exhausting it. The coffee stall (opposite), (pictorially well-sited and also, I imagine, one of the most strategically well-positioned of its kind in London) attracts a wonderfully mixed clientèle—market men, coppers, drivers, porters, off-beats, dead-beats, human flotsam and jetsam varied in the evenings by business-men and theatre-goers—the coffee stall's customers change according to the time of day or night. For the cost of a pie and a coffee or so you can have a ringside seat at a fruity Doolittle entertainment that cannot be matched elsewhere, yet visitors so often fail to avail themselves of it. They prefer to get famished, fagged out and thoroughly vexed by charging round the Horse Guards, Parliament Square and other insipid places in the belief that they are seeing London. The men's lavatory here is worth visiting, not only for its gaslit entrances, but also for its black-and-white and brown-and-white marble stalls, Victorian, by George Jennings & Co., and including the Royal Arms, the chequer board mosaic floor and the internal gas fittings; it is, in fact, an almost unspoiled period piece, at least until someone decides to modernise it.

And the market buildings themselves, dotted about with barrows, piles of boxes, piles of fruit and vegetables, and regularly patrolled by the market's official pigeons and cats are fascinating even at times when no business is being carried on, as on Saturday afternoons and Sundays. But the time to see it is in the early morning, when the lorries come lumbering in: by the time most people are having their breakfast, Covent Garden is jammed with barrows, lorries, porters, salesmen and buyers, in a confusion that seems incapable of ever being resolved; yet it is, some- how. If you have a great love affair on hand, you can say it with flowers from the Garden, as David Copperfield did on the important weekend when he went to declare himself to Dora.

'No walk in London, on a fine summer's day, is more agreeable than the passage through the flowers here at noon, when the roses and green leaves are newly watered,' said Leigh Hunt in one of his essays, 'and blooming faces come to look at them in those cool and shady avenues, while the hot sun is basking in the streets. On these occasions we were very well pleased with the market in its old state. The old sheds and irregular avenues, when dry, assorted well with the presence of leaves and fruits. They had a careless, picturesque look, as if a bit of an old sub- urban garden had survived from ancient times.

'Nothing, however, but approbation can be bestowed on the convenient and ele- gant state into which the market has been raised by the magnificence of the noble proprietor. . . . In time we hope to see the roofs of the new market covered with shrubs and flowers nodding over the balustrades . . . '

This is the market as it now stands, and, if you look at the pavilion on the S.W. corner, you can still read the inscription 'Jas Butler, seedsman, lavender water, etc.' who was there at the time Hunt wrote.

The chief attraction in Maiden Lane is, of course, Rules, one of the few genuine Victorian restaurants left. One of the few modifications since the 'nineties has been the appropriation of a part of the bar farthest from the door for dining: originally, the ground floor (opposite) was set apart for drinking. But the woodwork, plush, stained glass and the theatrical souvenirs remain intact. If you go upstairs, look for the stained glass door to the left, at the top of the staircase. This was put in for the convenience of Edward VII, a monarch who thought highly of the place. I believe it was at Rules and in the private room to which this door led that he had his quarrel with Lily Langtry. The English, being considerably less mouldy in those days, had no objection to the goings on of their merry monarch: I think his peccadilloes were a main ingredient in the popularity that allowed him to get away with anything, even his share in the Entente Cordiale, for which the English paid heavily.

Other items of interest in Maiden Lane include the old dairy; the delightful, early Victorian door incorporating the Royal Coat of Arms at the back of the

Adelphi Theatre; and the nineteenth-century herb shop of R. Brooks & Company, at the corner adjoining the magnificent Victorian offices of *The Lady*. Victorian classic at its best is a feature of the Covent Garden area; besides *The Lady* offices, the list includes the former premises of the Westminster Fire Office in King Street and the Garrick Club.

Connecting Maiden Lane with the Strand is a narrow alley, Bull Inn Court. There are bracket gas lamps on the walls, and ancient brickwork over the entrance at the Strand end, an entry that is lined with late Victorian tiling advertising the Adelphi Theatre and pointing the way 'To the Nell Gwynne Tavern'—a choice pub of vest pocket size and ancient date, one that still sold porter until fairly recent years.

Bedford Street—round the corner by Moss Bros—leads to New Row. The White

BEDFORDBURY

S.P...
Goodwins
Court

Swan is a Victorian pub with gilded and engraved glass and a nice stucco façade. Next to it is the old fashioned premises (Victorian below and eighteenth-century brick above) of Middlemass, the bakers. Lower down comes the Coliseum Dairy; note the churns and crates of bottles piled round the base of the lamp. It is, in fact, the lamps that give especial interest to this street, for there are four different types, the most recent being the 1910 pattern still fairly common in the area. But the two on the right-hand side as you go down—the two nearest St Martin's Lane —are very rare, especially the one which has a base of a stumpy and fluted Doric column, resembling the first pillar boxes.

Before the opening out of Trafalgar Square, St Martin's Lane ran alongside the portico of St Martin-in-the-Fields, a narrow lane for the whole of its length to the Strand. Not much of the architecture of that period remains—merely a fragment here and there, such as the Angel and Crown and Goodwin's Court. The latter is one of those surprises London keeps on hand to reward wanderers (opposite). It is a charming alley of bow-windowed houses, dating in its present form from the eighteenth century—good to look at, but rather noisy to live in—though perhaps not so noisy as it was when the whole area was bursting with human and animal life, the time when Dickens made Seven Dials and Monmouth Street the subjects of a couple of papers in the *Sketches by Boz*.

In those days, Monmouth Street was famous for its old clo'—there was at least one of these emporiums still in business in the 1940s. Dickens reconstructs the previous owners from their cast-off clobber, and speculates on their histories, deducing his biographical details from loud waistcoats, discarded top-boots and slovenly bonnets. Some of the old architecture remains above the shops. Indeed what is remarkable is that so much remains of the Dials (you can still trace the radiating pattern in its streets on a modern map) in spite of the efforts the Victorians made (by demolition and the cutting of New Oxford Street across the district) and the extensive post-war developments around St Giles's Circus. Shelton Street, full of old houses of the eighteenth and early nineteenth centuries, where the West End hamburger men stoke up, is a case in point, and proves the resilience the district has to change and modification.

'But the Dials are changing. There's no doubt about it,' said the manager of a contemporary-style bank on the edge of Seven Dials to me, not long ago. 'We used to have lots of prostitutes among our customers. Now we have hardly any.'

I said I was sad to hear it, for it was bad enough for the old clo' and junk shops to have gone from the Dials, without the bags going as well; it was calculated to make one head for the gin palace in despair.

However, it put me in mind of an encounter I once had with a prostitute late one evening in Covent Garden. It was in Bow Street, and I remember it as the only occasion on which I ever showed anything resembling wit or presence of mind. The lady invited me to come and talk to her, and on the instant the first verse of Goldsmith's poem, 'To Iris, in Bow Street, Covent Garden' flashed into my mind

—I suppose by association with the place. Accepting her invitation to talk, I said:

'Say, Iris, pretty rake
Dear mercenary beauty . . . '

That was as far as I got, for at that point she fled.

The first consecrated building to belong to Methodism was in West Street, Seven Dials. It still exists, a well-proportioned, plain, Georgian building, with round-headed windows and square-headed doors. It was originally a Huguenot chapel, until Wesley took it over in 1743. Today, it is used as a warehouse; of course, it ought to be restored and used once again as a place of Methodist worship. The contemporary style office block in St Martin's Lane is a poor exchange for May's Buildings and the adjoining eighteenth- and early nineteenth-century architecture that occupied the site until recent years. My drawing (pages 56/57) was done just before the demolition got under way: note the delightful façade with the pilaster strip treatment and the cornice with egg and dart moulding, all in cut brick, on the second house from the right.

Property of this kind, but much more exhausted, was demolished in the early years of the century to clear a site for the Coliseum, the most splendid music hall ever built in London. The Coliseum, opened in 1904, is by Frank Matcham, and is full of the bombast of Edwardian baroque. It is too coarse to be of much value architecturally, and the clutter of posters and signs that are part of its present-day use as a cinema do not help matters. In its career as a variety hall, it saw some remarkable occasions, including the visits of Bernhardt and Vesta Tilley's farewell performance in 1920.

In St Martin's Lane is the most perfect Victorian pub in London, apart from the Red Lion in St James's. This is, of course, the Salisbury, a theatrical pub, lovingly preserved in all its fin-de-siècle opulence and glitter, inside and out, marvellous in every way, rich in plush, engraved glass and mirrors and offering a late Victorian experience second to none. Cecil Court is round the corner, an alley devoted to second-hand book shops, but with a curio shop full of odds and ends from Egyptian tombs at the far end, where the cameo murder took place. Parallel to Cecil Court and a little farther along St Martin's Lane is St Martin's Court, a place of small shops, gas lamps and stage doors.

Its chief feature is Sheekey's, the Victorian fish restaurant with its old opal glass lamps still outside. In contrast to the ornate, full-blown Salisbury, J. Sheekey retains the air of an old-fashioned London dining-room. Photographs of a few of its famous customers and some Victorian family ones are all that Sheekey's goes in for in point of decoration, the proprietor holding to the old-fashioned belief that a restaurant is a place where you go for very good food.

Garrick Street leads to King Street, and so back to Covent Garden Market. The Garrick Club, already mentioned, was designed by Frederick Marrable and built in 1864; it is a late example of the Classic club-house of Pall Mall and St

James's, influenced, and by then at a considerable distance, by the Italian palaces of the Renaissance. The exterior, apart from the lamps, is the same now as it appears in the brightly-washed-in perspective of the front elevation in the possession of the club, though the stonework has become discoloured by the London smoke.

Almost opposite in Rose Street—Rose Street with its men's urinal in the angle of the wall, a rare early specimen—is the Lamb and Flag. When I first knew it, the pub still had its old stucco front, with a representation of the Agnus Dei in relief in a niche in the cornice. This ancient front—it was very decayed—was removed some years ago and replaced by a Georgian style façade. Fortunately, the interior is quite unchanged. It has an air of being well used and well liked. The old high wainscoting, low ceilings, mirror glass, the Gillray prints, the old photographs and playbills are as they have always been, and so are the willow-patterned beer pulls; the entire set up is a relief to eyes jaded by tarted up bar parlours, full of freak decor and antique oddments that were shipped in only yesterday.

Behind the Lamb is Floral Street. Langley Court, a narrow alley on the north side, is not much to look at nowadays, but until recent years it was an example of the way things manage to survive in London backwaters, by-passed by developments and left behind by progress, for the houses on one side were medieval; the gap left by their demolition is still there.

The Westminster Fire Office, who began business in Tom's Coffee House, St Martin's Lane, in 1717, moved into the impressive building in King Street in 1810, after the premises had been altered for the use of the company. The building was extended in 1857 when the Court Room, restored by Sir Albert Richardson in 1951, was built; some of the details of the façade, for example the cornice, seems to me to belong to this period (1857); it is characteristic of mid-Victorian classic at its best. Today, the company has moved elsewhere, but at present the façade is intact, including the splendid badge of the Company incorporating the portcullis from the arms of the City of Westminster and the feathers in compliment to the Prince of Wales (afterwards George II) who was a policy holder.

An interesting point in connection with the Westminster is that many of the most distinguished architects working in eighteenth-century London were directors of the company. The list includes John Crunden, the designer of Boodles Club and pupil of Henry Holland, also a director and the architect of Brooks Club; Chambers; Gibbs; and Flitcroft whose Church of St Giles-in-the-Fields, superbly restored after the war, is an essential item in a topographical tour of Seven Dials. The church is in the Palladian idiom as interpreted by Gibbs. Note the interesting Roman Doric gateway by Thomas Leverton, who designed some of the best domestic architecture in Bloomsbury.

Farther down King Street is the Essex Serpent, a market pub with an early licence. This wonderfully named pub has a Victorian Gothic façade, but the interior has been tidied and is somewhat disappointing. The tidying up process has been applied to the interior of the Opera Tavern (page 58) in Catherine Street, one of

my favourite Victorian relics on the far side of the market. The pub has some good plushy seats, engraved glass, playbills, aspidistra pots and cast iron tables, but it has also fake oil lamps and piped music and these things are hard to overlook. The façade is the ripest Victorian—an undisciplined mixture (and delicious because it is so) of all sorts of bits and pieces, mouldings of Greek origin or of no origin at all. Sir Albert Richardson once told me when I was a student that I was throwing away my talents and would never do any good if I persisted in admiring and drawing 'the wrong things' as he termed such examples as the Opera Tavern; perhaps he was right. Still, I have continued to admire debased designs of this kind without reserve or misgiving. Certainly no one has as yet rivalled, much less improved upon, the fully fledged pub architecture the Victorians arrived at in the late 1860s, nor is anyone likely to. What can be done, though, is to make sure they are taken seriously and carefully preserved in their entirety.

'Yes, I like the market,' said one of the off-beat wo-men who can be seen either drifting round the streets with bundles of papers or carrying out endless mathe-matical calculations in penny exercise books, 'Covent Garden agrees with me, and I sleep here, though I had a good education. But you've got to be careful. There are people around here with printing presses, and they're printing their own money . . . That's why they can afford to spend so much when everyone else is hard up. . . . You won't have a cork-tipped cigarette? No? Well, never mind. Next time you see me, I'll have finished my calculations, and I'll be able to tell you how it's done!'

VII

Wandering in Southwark

———————— * ————————

APART FROM THE GEORGE, the Cathedral and a slip along Bankside, including the Anchor, Southwark remains a closed book except to the more dedicated seekers after strange London flavours. The authors of wish-you-were-here post-cards find views of Southwark are not to be had, and the rubbernecks, though active enough on the opposite bank, seldom penetrate to the Surrey side. Perhaps the industrialisation which began in the nineteenth century puts them off. But the fact is that, though the ancient theatres and great coaching houses and inns (along with the prisons which made up the tri-partite character of the Borough) are gone for good—with, of course, the exception of the George, or that part of it which now remains—Southwark, properly studied and explored, will prove one of the most rewarding parts of London. Of course, one has to do it on foot.

Southwark makes a large contribution to the feeding of London. The stretch of warehouses for foodstuffs at the bridge foot and along Tooley Street has been justifiably named 'London's Larder', and there is also, of course, the Borough market. This has a character of its own with nothing of the suggestion of country gardens mingled with eighteenth-century gallantries we find at Covent Garden. The road through Southwark, the Borough High Street, was the way the market produce came in from Kent and Sussex to feed medieval London, and the market (to this day dealing mainly in fruit and vegetables) was established in the reign of Edward VI to regulate the trade.

Though utilitarian, the market has great interest and character; its site under the railway arches, sandwiched in, as it were, between the narrow streets that lead to Bankside and the Cathedral, ensures that. But there are still eighteenth-century buildings about, and piles of boxes, barrows and baskets (page 65) under the gas lamps and ancient cast iron bollards; and though the continual rumble of the railway overhead is all but deafening, you can hear above the noise of railway and market the song of blackbirds in the Cathedral garden.

Bankside can easily be visited from the market. Items of interest including the Anchor, recently extended—the new parts looking even older than the original, the green-tiled gents opposite, the Clink bollards and, next to the Anchor, the firm which specialises in breaking eggs. You see the staff in their white overalls at mid-day, women mostly, having a breather from this most curious profession of egg-

59

breaking. Besides the old houses now used by the Cathedral clergy, there is the Cardinal's House, said, very hopefully, to be a residence of Wren during the building of St Paul's (Wren actually lived in Idol Lane). Anna Lee, the film star, lived at the Cardinal's House during the 1930s; at that time Bankside was cobbled, and during week-days always crowded with horse-drawn vehicles.

The Power Station was then the City of London Electric Lighting Company. With the demolition of the old station several interesting old streets, such as White Hind Alley and Pyke Gardens, disappeared, and so did the foreshoremen, called 'mudlarks', like the nineteenth-century street arabs who dived for pennies. The job of the foreshoremen was to clear mud from the shore where the coal barges berthed, and they worked in shifts according to the tides. In addition to their wages, they were entitled to a 'stocking allowance' to cover wear and tear on the thick sewermen's type of stocking they wore beneath their waders.

Most of the interest of Southwark is, however, centered on the High Street. The George is, I think, too well known to be mentioned here, but note the Victorian premises of W. H. & H. Le May, hopfactors, next to Lloyds Bank at the corner of the George's inn yard—a stucco front, the top half of which consists of a charming bas relief, with figures of a youth and a maiden somewhat in the Walter Crane manner, picking the hops which surround the lettering in the centre.

On the other side of the road, behind the war memorial, is a picturesque remnant of ancient Southwark—the medieval cottage enclosed by eighteenth-century houses in Calvert's Buildings (opposite). It reminds me always of a remark Dickens makes of an old house that seemed to have got itself in a corner, and got lost, when it was a young house and couldn't find its way out again.

Wander in Calvert's Buildings and you feel yourself suddenly transformed to one of the antique streets of some cathedral town, such as Salisbury or Canterbury, though the Victorian offices of the hop firms press in on all sides, and the fumes and noise of modern Southwark are only a few yards distant through the archway.

On the other side of the High Street is a recent arrival in Southwark, and one entirely to my taste. This is a vintners, the Boot and Flogger. I haven't the remotest notion what a flogger is, unless it is a version of that war-time character, the spiv. There, if you have not already eaten at the George, you can sample a variety of cheeses, ham, smoked salmon, savouries and coffee as well as wine. The style is that of a Victorian coffee house, the interior being snugly curtained off from the street and supplied with Windsor chairs, posters relating to London Bridge and its neighbourhood, a period cash register, storm lamps and a sanded floor. They set you at ease at the Boot and Flogger; there is no suggestion of hurry—an attitude opposed to that of many modern eating-places where the aim seems to be to make you uncomfortable, so you will not be tempted to take up valuable space for more than a few necessary minutes. I pronounce it one of the most satisfactory experiences in London, the Flogger.

While writing this chapter, a real-life flogger presented himself to me in South-

wark, in the pleasing Victorian pub, so charmingly named the Blue Eyed Maid, farther along the High Street—a successor to the inn of the same name referred to by Dickens. The flogger was himself Dickensian, for a closer resemblance to the great Micawber I have never beheld, and flogging intercoms was his line of business.

'My customers,' he said, as he produced his wares, 'are mainly licensed houses and ladies' hairdressers. It will only take me a few seconds to demonstrate.'

'Vy,' said a character of vintage aspect, rather like a cabby, 'don'tcher try the bookies, the betting shops? Nah, you'd fink they'd go fer yer walkie-talkie in a big way.'

'Oddly enough, sir,' said Micawber, 'I've never succeeded with them. There

61

may be some special reason for this, or there may not. I cannot tell. Opinions may differ as to why turf accountants—which you rightly term betting shops—do *not* go for two-way intercoms, guaranteed unreservedly for a year, in a big way. But persistent exploring of this potential market has, in my case, led to negative results; in a word, I've drawn a blank.'

Another Victorian pub is the Crown, a fine example of nineteenth-century stucco, with crowns in the infilling above the windows and another and larger one in the curved pediment above the cornice. St George's Church, restored after war damage in 1952, is by John Price, and dates from about 1735. The tower gives distinction to the otherwise mainly nondescript architecture of the street. Little Dorrit was baptised and married in this church; it was on its steps that she was found by the verger early one morning, having been locked out of the Marshalsea Prison. She appears in the new east window, a small figure with a poke bonnet, her hands in prayer. St George's is fortunately free from the darkening effects of much stained glass, hence the interior is a cool, light and airy refuge from the grinding of traffic and the dirt of the streets. The ceiling, slightly theatrical in a way difficult to define, is a replica of the one put up in the nineteenth century and damaged by the bombing. It was designed by Basil Champneys in 1897, and, far from being a mere pastiche, is a graceful and convincing essay in an Italianate vein. Champneys, whose most famous work is the Rylands Library, Manchester, was an architect of individual quality, whose work deserves more study and appreciation. The ceiling of St George's, with its heads of cherubs breaking through a cloudy sky, comes as a surprise to those familiar only with his Gothic work. The best view of St George's is from the corner of Lant Street, looking towards London Bridge; from this point, the combination of sturdiness and elegance in the design of the tower and spire can be seen to advantage, and there is a bit of old property to the right which assists in framing the composition.

Lant Street, incidentally, is nothing nowadays; all the old property that Dickens and Bob Sawyer knew when they lived there has gone; a great block of flats dominates what is now merely a site or a name, but just short of Lant Street and on the High Street is an interesting pair of old houses, a relic of seventeenth-century Southwark, once the offices of the Distil Coffee Company.

Trinity Square, a turning off the Borough High Street, possesses one of the finest neo-Grecian churches in London. Neither a description nor an illustration can do justice to the refined proportions and the integrity and austerity of a design that combines scholarship with a rare delicacy of feeling, entirely avoiding the heaviness and dullness that characterises so much neo-Classic architecture. The tower above the pediment, with a top storey based on the Tower of the Winds, is particularly satisfying (opposite). Holy Trinity, built in 1823-4, is by Bedford, architect of several of the best South London churches of that period including St John's in the Waterloo Road.

It is seen at its best on one of those sunlit evenings the late spring or early summer brings to London, when the light changes the honey-coloured stone of the lower part of the church into amber, and the tower into a splendid golden thing, with violet-blue shadows. At the time of writing, Holy Trinity (incidentally the church referred to in Tom Costello's song) is empty, though not uncared for: no one seems to know what to do with it now the parishioners have been scattered. It might be a good idea—not necessarily one that would pay—to use it for its original purpose. Certainly the building ought to be preserved; and Trinity Square with it, for the whole forms one of the most visually satisfying architectural arrangements in South London.

Behind St George's is a relic that no wanderer in the Borough ought to miss. Take the narrow entry called Angel Place close to the Crown: from a point half way down to the end of the alley are the remains of the notorious Marshalsea Prison, a nick where Dickens' father was imprisoned for debt, to the novelist's lasting chagrin. The remains of the prison are among flats, and the local children play under the grim sloping walls, their red and green lollies making a touch of bright colour against the ancient brickwork.

Several of the iron-barred windows, painted a faded blue, remain, and, though the portions of the prison still existing are not extensive, there is sufficient to leave an impression of melancholy—say on a windy, rainswept day in winter—that one is not likely easily to forget. I was meditating on all this, and thinking of Little Dorrit's childhood within its great grey walls, while wandering round the district recently, when I pulled up outside the window of a sweet and toy shop. The shop was modern, with nothing of any special character to attract my attention, apart from a printed notice stuck on the glass. This announcement was in Victorian type —not the Victorian type now so fashionable among designers and commercial artists, but the real thing, well used and smudgy, without doubt the stock of some local jobbing printer whose firm had bought the type in the 1880s or earlier, and had been using it in the ordinary way of business ever since. And it read:

Tops and Whips

are in

1/6

There was more in that notice than met the eye. Being interpreted, it provided clear evidence that the London season is not yet consigned to the rubbish heap— the London season, that is, of the back alley and Casey Court kids, with its traditional street games, each, by some mysterious dispensation, in its appointed place in the calendar—an arcane knowledge that unhappily passes with childhood. Besides this, the notice seemed to me to affirm the longevity and persistence of simple things. In an age of Batman, spacemen and God-knows-what-next men and a co-ordinated effort to sell pop music, pop foods, pop fads and all the

64

revolting razmataz of American life to English children—at an increasingly early age—it seemed to assert the virtues of old-hat pastimes and to assume that there were still children who hadn't been got at, processed, modulated and persuaded by educators and ad-men; it was what a South Bank cleric would call a challenge.

These ideas received what I hope was further confirmation at London Bridge. There was a grubby little boy with a pudding basin haircut one used to see in the bad old days cadging for pennies by means of a little mongrel dog, appealingly gazing from a cardboard box. I gave him a coin, and said I hoped he was looking after the dog properly. He said, yes, mister, he was, and the dog always came out with him for pennies; it was wot the dog liked doing best. I said, well give him my regards, and while you're about it, tell him that tops and whips are in. It's important, I said, and don't you forget it.

VIII

Around King's Cross

— * —

I HAVE ALWAYS CONGRATULATED MYSELF on having lived for two or three years in the neighbourhood of St Pancras and King's Cross Stations, especially the former, for St Pancras, besides being a great monument both to steam locomotion (which we ought never to have given up) and to the Gothic Revival, is also the only work of art produced by Scott. At Worcester College—remembering the Frenchman's punning remark about the chapel's not being a railway station—he was unforgivable; elsewhere he was either correct or deadly academic, sometimes both, a purveyor of architecture that refused to come alive. But at St Pancras he was inspired—that is the only word for it—to produce a work of art that almost rivals in quality the supreme achievement of Victorian Gothic, the Manchester Town Hall.

After the publication of my *London Nobody Knows*, in which I mentioned the grandly dramatic and, indeed, poetic silhouette of the station seen from Pentonville (opposite), I had a most interesting letter from Mr Michael Waterhouse, grandson of the architect of Manchester Town Hall and himself an architect. He wrote to tell me of a small pen-watercolour drawing his father had made in 1889 from this spot at the corner of Penton Street.

Architects, as I have said, were artists once—a long time ago—and skilled in the art of watercolour painting, and moreover they were not too busy or too proud to draw other people's buildings. 'A lovely misty autumn view of the fairy scene,' is how Mr Waterhouse described it, and that is precisely what this distant view, almost unchanged in a century, is; there is something about those pinnacles and crested roofs that lifts up the spirits, like a patch of sunlight far out at sea or on distant uplands. I have never been able to understand how it was that Scott, at other times so dully accomplished and pedestrian, could create this wonderful building, for wonderful it is, inside and out, if only you can forget the snack bars, the advertisements, the modern trains—utterly, devastatingly wrong—and all the rest of the modern paraphernalia which tends to reduce the extreme visual pleasure projected, as it were, from this building on all sides, in all its details, elevations and surfaces. I have been visiting and studying St Pancras almost weekly since I left its neighbourhood—almost two decades—and am only now beginning to feel that I know and appreciate it as it ought to be known and appreciated.

Another mystery is why the visitors who emerge from one of its great dramatic dark entrances ever go further. They are here on holiday: St Pancras ought to be their holiday. Nothing more is needed, for the station itself provides all that sight seeing could require. They ought to spend their week or fortnight climbing the great staircase (still with its original carpet), staring up at the magnificent façade, eating the capitals, letting the Victorian Gothic spirit sink into their weary, travel-stained bodies. That is one good argument for the re-opening of the hotel which occupies (or occupied) most of the main façade from the first-floor level until 1935. But the great and splendid fireplaces of baronial proportions, the tiled rooms, carved doors and some of the original furniture still survives; the thing is to pull down the partitions, clear the offices out and re-establish this sumptuously, truly romantic hotel, taking care to give the chambermaids an extra allowance in return for wearing frills and lace caps with streamers down their backs. In fact, the whole of the station—hotel, platforms, trains, refreshment rooms and the station approach—ought to be restored to its original appearance, irrespective of whether this course would pay or not. For, quite apart from the fact that accountancy has far too much influence in present day life, St Pancras is a work of art, and considerations of profit and loss are therefore irrelevant. Even if they were not, a sum of money inconsiderable to the country could restore and rehabilitate the place in a fitting manner, down to the small details of period weighing and chocolate machines, porters' uniforms and the like—with an infinitely greater degree of profitability than that which we now realise on the astronomical sums spent on hideous armaments, scientific research, the bolstering up of pettifogging regimes that hate us and the insatiable appetite of the Welfare State.

There are several reasons why St Pancras is supreme among the buildings by Scott. For one thing, its site, previously occupied by the slums of Agar Town, is a commanding one, as far as its frontage on the Euston Road is concerned, and Scott made the fullest use of his opportunity. Second, the fact that the design has an inner harmony, extending to all its parts; a harmony that reaches to the great train shed by Barlow behind, a brilliant feat of engineering, perfectly integrated into Scott's Gothic work. Third, the completely satisfying shapes the building makes considered purely as a mass; the way it produces endlessly varying silhouettes when seen from no matter what distance or angle—on either the short or the long axis—and finally the vitality of Scott's detailing and the quality of the materials, mostly from the Midlands, used in the construction.

Scott put the same care, though in a plainer manner, into those parts of the station concerned with its important goods traffic. If you compare the correct carving of Scott's church porch in Cornhill (clapped on to existing work by Wren and very fairly typical of Scott) you will see at once that, either as the result of Ruskin's influence or a study of French and, especially, Italian Gothic, Scott infused a liveliness of handling into his carved work at St Pancras which sets it apart from his usual pedestrian manner. The sculptures of the capitals of the great porch—grotesque birds and acanthus leaves—have a vitality hardly inferior to

the Venetian and Lombardic originals. Incidentally, the coffered ceiling of this porch is chronically in need of attention, for hardly any vestiges of its original painted ornament are left. It is, as I have said, a building to be seen in the round, and the complete tour should include the men's lavatory, which still has many of its original features, including the Gothic windows and tiles. There is a running border of an Early English pattern, white on blue, and the walls above are tiled with a drop repeat of a snowflake pattern, the snowflake motif being blue on white. Examine also the linenfold panelling and the capitals of Victorian engine-drivers in the booking-hall, and take a last look at the building from the corner of the Caledonian Road—a magnificent view with the clock tower in the foreground.

After a study of St Pancras, and before touring its immediate area, I recommend refreshment at Reggiori's (above) a snack bar but with its sumptuous Edwardian interior almost unchanged. The mosaic floor is chipped and cracked, and the lino has seen better days. Modern tables and chairs and a snack counter have been moved in, but the walls, ceilings and stained glass remain wonderfully untouched. The panelled ceiling is of tile and wood, with hexagons infilled with arabesque scroll-work, and the hanging lamps are art nouveau originals. Bevel-edged mirrors are inset into the tiled walls. Between each mirror is a thin, tall panel of a Walter Crane flavour—pale grey-green leaves and red camellia-like flowers on a yellow ground. From the walls, brass coat hangers hold out their arms pleadingly; they

will accept your cloth cap and muffler, though they were bred to take silk hats and curly-brimmed bowlers. The mirrors will reflect your reach-me-down, plastic-mackintoshed modernity equally faithfully—except, perhaps, for a faint cloud on their surface—but they were used to reflecting big flowery hats at one time, high collars and waxed moustaches. Besides a quantity of stained glass, there is elaborate plasterwork in the spandrils of the arcades, and a richly carved staircase leads to the regions below.

When I was at University College and lived in Cartwright Gardens, Reggiori was still in his old à-la-carte order; you sat on bentwood chairs, and in the middle of each white tablecloth was a combined flower holder and cruet stand. What's more, the waitresses wore their black crêpe-de-chine dresses and white caps. Though these reassuring features are gone, it is still possible to reconstruct Reggiori's Edwardian past—at least until someone decides to knock down the lot. In my student days, and in fact until within the last year or so, there was a genuine chop-house in the area—near to the King's Cross Post Office: Adams's Chop House, it styled itself, and went in for tempting viands in the window, and pots of fern. This also has become a snack-bar, but the word 'Adams' still remains on the wall and so does the cast-iron bracket that once supported a gas lamp.

Thus refreshed, one is ready for the grand tour of the Caledonian Road, an experience that may be likened to a study in greys and low tones, high-lighted in places by funeral parlours, coin-operated laundries and betting shops. But first make a detour to see the delightful early nineteenth-century houses of Lloyd Square, part of the well-kept Lloyd Baker Estate which slopes down to the King's Cross Road. The square (early nineteenth-century) and some of its approaches (Lloyd Baker Street and Wharton Street) consist of small semi-detached villas with Grecian pediments, all in a simple and homely but severe style; cottage architecture of a type absolutely right for London; notice how well the vines and rambler roses combine with the architecture, to produce what on summer evenings appears like a romantic illustration from Loudon or P. F. Robinson. Lloyd Square is intact on three sides the fourth being a late Victorian school which does not seriously interrupt the unpretentious harmony of the terraced groups.

The detailing of the mouldings is extremely simple, the austerity of the effect being relieved by the iron railings. My drawing (opposite) was made from the corner of St Helena Street, with a greenhouse in the foreground full of ferns, ivies and flowering plants all within a couple of minutes of King's Cross. Cumberland Gardens, a flagged passage of delightful houses is even more remarkable. No. 3 was the home of Eric Newton, the art critic and designer. The entrance step has been enlivened by a mosaic, in which the owner has adroitly turned an inconvenient coal-hole cover into a sun by surrounding it with refulgent rays. Cumberland Gardens in the spring, when the prunus and almonds are out, and the thrushes and blackbirds of the neighbourhood are tuning up, is as delightful as any Chelsea backwater; it seems unbelievable that King's Cross is so close, but once you have got past the splendid Italianate Percy Arms, the crumbling terraces and faded balconies assure you there has been no mistake.

The round trip of the Caledonian Road reaches takes no more than a couple of hours, and it affords a backward-looking view of the London of Sickert. Most of it—at least enough to disrupt the gaunt harmony of the district—will have been destroyed in a few years' time by those who, under the impression that plumbing and other amenities are sufficient unto the day, are bent on rebuilding the so-called obsolete, outdated areas. Perhaps they will be satisfied by the time London has been turned into a second Rotterdam. Meanwhile, there are still peeling terraces and industrial prospects to be enjoyed, in which the human element is still in the same key; you may still encounter people linked arm in arm, singing in the street, having had too much to drink, and there is no lack of mournful old men and red-faced middle-aged men with greyhounds. Galvanised baths are still on sale at the ironmongers, and a good thing too, for there is nothing wrong in boiling water and taking your bath in front of the kitchen range. It is certainly better than being skied to the top of a multi-storey block, a prey to loneliness, claustrophobia and Welfare State busy-bodies.

Keystone Crescent, at the beginning of the Caledonian Road, should not be missed: it is a very unexpected and surprising backwater of nice old early nineteenth-century cottages, with tubs of plants here and there. A chimney sweep lives in the middle, and the whole affair is sound old-time London working class, as yet uninvaded by the Venetian blind and blue door brigade. Behind the crescent is Northdown Street with a fine, but neglected terrace of stock brick. The form and proportions place it well within the Georgian tradition. Emphasis is given to the centre by Ionic pilaster strips and a raised triangular pediment, and the flanking wings on either side have well designed, rectangular-headed doors, supported by Doric columns.

Farther along, the Caledonian Road crosses the canal, and here are industrial landscapes every bit as good as those of Salford stretching out in both directions, my favourite being the row of small houses perched above the dandelion- and rag-wort-covered bank of the canal and separated from it by a leaning fence; a factory chimney and a gas lamp give additional character to the composition, which is rounded off by the distant dark arch with giant brick voissoirs through which the canal disappears.

Past Copenhagen Street, on the right, is a row of magnificent, peeling, stuccoed terraced houses, where kids scream in neglected gardens full of chickweed and old, wet newspapers, a place of lace curtains and peering heads. The stucco has almost entirely departed from the cracked gate piers which lean along the terrace at a variety of angles; of the urns that once topped them, one only remains, a fragment of a vanished civilisation, like an amphora dug up on a building site. Then come the shops built out in front of the old terraces—the TV and refrigerator shops, with special offers, the drug stores, furniture shops with settees parked

VOTE MOSS

St Pancras
from York Way

out on the pavement like stranded whales, the betting shops and undertakers with funerals to suit all pockets, and past them weaves a continuous frieze of old men and old women, housewives, prams and kids.

You turn off to the Caledonian Market up Market Road, a little way beyond Pentonville. The White Horse, a large square pub in the Italian style, one of the four similar buildings that once stood on the four corners of the market, surveys over its balcony a most melancholy sight. Once you could buy anything, animate or inanimate, that the human heart with its need for possessions could crave. Today the blocks of flats are creeping over that vast site, catching up with the rank grass and ragwort. Grass also grows between the paving stones of the Market Road, and luxuriates up the faded blue iron railings, as if in some Venetian island deserted since the time of the Doges, and living on memories. The clock in the market tower, still counting out the hours, is a symbol of a retreat from the times when a coster setting up in business bought his donkey there, where he sold it again if the enterprise failed to come up to scratch; where Londoners could furnish their entire house in one go, on the spot, from attic to area; a vanished life that has its memorial in that most interesting book *A Pitch on the Stones*. One pities the kids, playing in the rubble, as the blocks advance like an army on the march, though they will never realise what they have missed by being born far too late.

York Way has a dispiriting melancholy fully equal to the café, undertaker and serve-yourself pessimism of the Caledonian Road. It is a thoroughfare of thundering lorries, dust, engineering shops, railway walls and dockleaves. Tucked in a corner by the railway is an oasis for the tired and thirsty traveller in the shape of an agreeable Victorian pub, the Fortune of War, with sand-blasted glass doors having the legend Bottles and Jugs—also a survival from the days before yesterday.

All the way along, as you approach the canal, come the old men of the pavements, apparently lost in thought, each a mystery even to himself and most wearing huge cloth caps. These flat cloth caps, some with a button in the centre, a style favoured by Edwardian navvies, are interesting, for the old men's ears act as consoles or brackets to keep the cap from descending over their watery eyes. And finally you have the reward of all dedicated travellers in this uncharted region—the dreaming spires of St Pancras (on the previous page). From this distance, the station reminds me of those fairy palaces drawn in my childhood by Charles Folkard and Anne Anderson, or like the ones Burne Jones pictured, in the depths of old and mysterious woods. Sometimes the pinnacles and spires are touched with a dying September light that transmutes the railway station into the City of God that Bunyan saw beyond the Delectable Mountains.

IX

Meditations in Carnaby Street

————————— ✳ —————————

I CONFESS that, with certain reservations and misgivings, I am much in favour of Swinging London, in spite of the fact that its existence has been denied by some commentators, who claim it to be no more than a myth imposed by journalists, models and cult photographers on the square inhabitants of Dragsville. But it exists right enough, flamboyant, multi-coloured, lively, tasteless, dubious; a corny renaissance with an inner misgiving, containing the built in germs of its own dissolution, and made possible only by the money the younger generation has to spend, giving them, largely by means of clothes, a fictitious sense of purpose that these disoriented hippies had hitherto lacked.

And the superclothes, heirs at a distance of the flash clothes of the fifties, gave the hipsters a local habitation besides: Kings Road, Chelsea, at first, and then Carnaby Street, each with its Saturday morning parade of mods and swinging dolls. Today the boutiques are opening up in Fouberts Place, round the corner from Carnaby Street, and in places as far from the usual haunts of the scenesmen as Edgware Road and in the London suburbs. Carnaby Street is now self-conscious, tourist-haunted. It is as full of American accents as it is of discotheque jazz and pop colour, and this may mean that only the second-rate swingers will stay there: the way out ones will clap on their spats and granny specs and seek new areas of action. For the moment, the rubber-necks go to goggle; it is the thing to go to Carnaby Street, and have your photograph taken to prove it to the folks back home either in Birmingham, Warwickshire, or Birmingham, Alabama. It's the trend. Moreover, these ancients—that is to say, anyone over twenty-five—are themselves on the rag-trade bandwagon—the spending end of it—and endeavour to postpone the onset of middle age (this applies especially to men) by purchasing clothes originally designed with youngsters in mind.

Fouberts Place, a narrow lane off Regent Street, was at one time not unlike a side-street in a country town: it was a place of old-fashioned tobacconists and newsagents, full of steady old boys and steady old girls, unchanged, it seemed, for a century. Now it has joined the swingers, and it is here that you will find Lord Kitchener's Valet—not without precedent, either, for the alley is named after Comte Foubert, a refugee from the French Revolution, who started a fencing academy and later a riding school in order to earn a living (page 77). Lord Kitchener's Valet announces himself and his stock of mod cons to the jeansmen by means of a stuffed gorilla who jerks a Union Jack this way and that from an upper window. There is also a hanging sign, realistically painted in the pub tradition, of Kitchener's head, accompanied by those gloved fingers, like a bunch of bananas, from the Great War poster that pointed the way to the New Armies and slaughter in Flanders. Only, the youngsters who crowd the shop to buy new and secondhand uniforms, cocked hats, faked medals and other kinky gear have not the slightest intention of belonging to an army—new or old. A sour old person might consider they want the uniform without the discipline: if so, they—the youngsters—are quite right.

Not all the old squares are up to the uniform craze. I was behind an old couple in the Strand, and they were walking behind a young clothesman wearing a vivid scarlet jacket, striped trousers and jackboots; they were wondering how the Army allowed his sidewhiskers and shoulder-length hair; they were wondering what the army was coming to. Lord Kitchener's Valet has rows of such outfits, gold-braided, brass-buttoned, with peaked caps, badges and cloaks to match, though the ready-to-wear dandyism that results from dressing up in this rig is rather that of Nathan and Ruritania than of a military tailor and Wellington Barracks. Some of the faddists add a beaver hat à la Pickwick or a lace cravat to their military gear—with striking results. Lord Kitchener—or, at least, his valet—reverses the accepted conventions of merchandising, for his windows are entirely obscured—in contrast to the time-honoured philosophy of shovelling in all you've got—apart from small keyhole shapes through which you have to peer. Inside, the hussar-like jackets and the military-style cloaks occupy one wall, and there are more below, down the spiral staircase, and pith helmets, also, to keep the London sun off your soft head, posters, op (or pop) watches, old postcards, Union Jack cushions with the Field Marshal's portrait in the middle and other nutty items for the furnishing of your room or pad.

Much of this kinky gear and a lot of the clothes on which the youngsters spend so much of their money is interchangeable between the sexes. Such considerations would give Kitchener cause for alarm, and he would surely jib at the Granny specs, however low the physical standard required by the New Armies. He would consider them an insult to the flag.

Lord Kitchener is not the only trendsman in the street; there are other boutiques selling the new male fashions—art nouveau shirts, shirts with laced collars and cuffs, American Civil War style caps, vivid jackets and jeans—but he is the most visually entertaining if only because of his flag-wagging gorilla, from which, along with the fake medals and other spoof military bits and pieces, we infer a certain irreverence to our late lamented Empire, on which the sun has at last set. It gives one food for thought, as the sombrero-hatted, mini-skirted chicks pass up and down, ogling from under their false eyelashes the very latest thing in a Victorian frockcoat and a surprising waistcoat—a latter-day dandy, a Corinthian of Carnaby

I was Lord Kitcheners Valet
Fouberts Place.

Street, whom you might mistake for Disraeli, until he opens his mouth. Here comes a Civil War veteran from the army of the Potomac, heavily bearded and with a swagger that would have made General Grant look like 10 cents—and Confederate cents, at that. He has got an edge on the others, this veteran, and as he passes the dollies, they give him approving glances, though he never fired a shot in anger and the bullet holes in his denim sleeve are self-inflicted.

Two dollies have come up to me as I draw, the swashbuckling veteran passing the three of us on his way to where the action is—in Carnaby Street—and I ask them what they think of him.

'He's the tops for being geary.'

'He's beat, man, he's beat, and he's the most.'

'We mean he's the greatest, the most in gear who ever was.'

I am trying to overcome my faintheartedness in order to ask for further elucidation—a more specific analysis suitable to my squared up comprehension—but the attention of the dollies is already wandering, for coming into view, a face among the crowd, is a youth in a velvet suit, with a high starched collar sprouting from below. His headgear is a Pickwick hat. All told, he has a fairly complete resemblance to the Mad Hatter; but for one thing, and that is a pair of large glasses with Union Jacks in the lenses. I ask the dollies how they rate him. They say they rate him high, very high. In fact, they say he is the very latest, and I cannot help seeing the justice of their verdict.

You can view these kinky kings of Carnaby Street almost any afternoon. All you do is join the throng on the pavements, and leave the rest to the mods. You may find someone dressed like John Bull, with a Union Jack waistcoat, for, in the matter of sartorial swing, honest John (always dipping his hands in his pockets and shelling out) was in the groove long before Lord Kitchener ever had a valet, though in these days he has become somewhat old hat and has been made to eat humble pie and generally kicked up the backside. If not John Bull, then you may meet John Peel, but you will never, on any consideration, meet a youth dressed as John Citizen, for he is too much like your square old Dad: in fact he is your Dad with all his imperfections on his head, and too dull to be imitated.

I cannot think this wearing of military toggery means anything. Or, if it does, then its sole significance is that the fad is a handy way of providing yourself with an individuality you do not in fact possess—until you put your gear on. Most likely, though, the simple explanation is the correct one—that military togs are being worn because others are wearing them. But one aspect of this jeanage dressing up that seems to me to be capable of analysis in some depth is the mentality of those youngsters who frequent a certain merchant in the East End in order to be fitted out with College and University colours they are not entitled to wear—even in a permissive society. There is something rather depressing about it, for no one taking a second glance at these youngsters would mistake them for undergraduates, red brick or otherwise. Like the Saturday morning promenaders of Carnaby Street and the Kings Road, they come from the desolate suburbs, from the soul-destroying uniformity of the great and terrible housing estates. They are shop girls, typists, unskilled building trade workers, pathetically trying to prove something, to kid somebody.

There is nothing wholly new in this, though elaborately staged self-deception belonged mainly to the middle-aged London failures at one time. I used to live in a boarding house full of these Walter Mittys and old pretenders. Some were name-droppers, others were arm-chair adventurers; they were passionate lovers who would have screamed if a woman had gone anywhere near them, and one wore a natty blazer with an elaborate badge and a Latin motto that translated gave the show away: 'Study at Home for Success'. In time, one develops a liking for these duds with an infinite capacity for illusion, and acknowledges a certain artistry about their fantasy world.

All this, however, is keeping us from savouring Carnaby Street, which is waiting round the corner of Fouberts Place—a dazzling combination of beat and pop noises, strident colour and erotic but deadpan humanity, which only the strongest-minded can sample without the use of tranquilisers. Carnaby Street is only short, and even so part of it is taken up by the premises of the 'St James and Pall Mall Electric Light Company 1897'. What is left is not so distinguished architecturally, but it packs a punch. There are only two old shops—the ironmongers and the old tobacconists—and even they, the tobacconists, have taken to putting a discreet Carnaby Street label on some of their fancy goods.

Pugh's Place, a narrow alley by the side of the ironmongers, affords the strongest possible contrast to the jazzmataz of the rest of the swinging street; it is composed of crumbling old property almost at the last stage of exhaustion, with a projecting gas lamp on a corner.

That the Carnaby Street boutiques, male, female and epicene, have effected a dividend-paying revolution is certain. It is equally certain that the young owners and designers of these work harder and take more chances than their poor-spirited elders ever did, but a few turns up and down the street—once you have assured yourself you are not in some uneasy dream—and the correction forces itself on you that however rebellious the mods may appear, they are in reality as dull and as processed, as tame and as conforming as their suburban parents. Their blank expressionless faces cancel out the message of the clothes; clothes that, proposing a break from uniformity, have themselves become uniforms. If it be a revolution, it is the tamest that ever was. It is one without convictions, let alone without barricades, and carried on by puppets on strings. Nonetheless, the young-hearted middle-aged weave in and out of the shops with their newly acquired clothes. The Americans photograph each other and everyone else, endlessly, the English visitors crowd into Gear and the music goes round and round.

Gear is a lively, interesting shop, full of objects of hippie culture, such as psychedelic posters of a debased art nouveau pattern from San Francisco, old ginger beer bottles, scarlet women cushions, enamel ware, Edwardian jerries ('The Good Companion Anti-Splash Thunderbowl' with an eye in the centre) and an old wooden counter with an old Fry's chocolate display case. Gear issue their own posters—reprints of nineteenth-century ones. These and other items are much to my taste. But there was an object I saw in the window one day in spring 1967 which gave me food for thought—more so, perhaps, than the rest of the street. This was a figure made from a mop. It stood on a brass bedstead, and was labelled 'I am the Risen Christ'. Now, there was a time (surely?) when ordinary men and women would have been disquieted, even horrified. I saw no sign of this among the crowds: in fact, they were amused and it was this that I found so uncommonly distressing. For it seems to me that hiving off one's stuffinesses is one thing, and mock-Christs quite another. It seems to me that faithless clerics, mini-skirts, sexual revolution, shots in the arm and the rest of it, though apparently unconnected, are in reality all part of the same thing, and that London, the swinging city, is only an effect and not a cause. It seems to me that Kitchener—the real one 'of Khartoum'—square as he undoubtedly was, might after all have had more oil in his can than we nowadays admit; and it also seems to me that, if he were able to return to the scene, he might well call for a Good Companion Anti-Splash Thunderbowl, and promptly use it to some purpose. It seems so to me, though no doubt today's jeanagers, when retired from the scene, will develop the same nostalgia for Carnaby and the other swinging streets as those of my generation have for Charlotte Street and Soho.

In fact, Carnaby Street is already passing into folklore. One Sunday morning recently in Petticoat Lane, I encountered a weedy youth with a bundle of plastic reproductions of the Carnaby Street nameplate, 'City of Westminster, Carnaby Street W.1'. He was rapidly disposing of them, and his message to the appreciative customers was, 'Don't forgitcher genuine plastic nameplates. Every one real plastic and guaranteed. Most famous street on earth. Yer genuine plastic, smooth surface, name plates. Only a few left. Carnaby Street, ladies, in the heart of swingin' London . . . Carnaby Street, ladies, with the real plastic surface, the smooth surface, in the heart of swingin' London'.

X

Around Charing Cross

———— * ————

'I TALKED of the cheerfulness of Fleet Street, owing to the constant quick succession of people which we perceive passing through it. J OHNSON. "Why, Sir, Fleet Street has a very animated appearance; but I think the full tide of human existence is at Charing Cross".'

That reply of Johnson's seems to have a magnificent xenophobia about it, unless I am mistaken—a Baroque insularity of no common order. Johnson pays no attention to the life—at full tide or otherwise—in foreign capitals; instead, with

81

a homing instinct equal to that of the pigeons of the area, he places the vortex of existence on this planet firmly where we can all see it—at Charing Cross. Paris, Rome, Berlin, St Petersburg: you might have thought that they, too, had their vortices: but they are all places of slack water: the full tide is at Charing Cross.

I think of this phrase each time I loiter along the paved area on the Northern side of Trafalgar Square, looking at the sunlight through the spray of the fountains, admiring the iridescent colour on the breasts of the pigeons and wondering why the visitors cast by this tide (as it seems) into Trafalgar Square are unable to float off again to see more unusual sights that lie only a short distance away. And I think of the lions who used to frequent the square before those bronze ones by Landseer took up residence a century ago—before there was any tide of human existence—before the pigeon corn and souvenir men, even. The remains of these lions can still be seen. Thought of in conjunction with the present day life of the square, they force devilishly unpleasant reflections on the mind, relative to the depths of time—ideas that are not easily erased. Any fossil will have that effect— even the living fossils who haunt the museums and tea-shops wearing old macs and holding paper carriers—but the Trafalgar Square relics are, I think, the most potent in London. They are on display in Drummond's Bank—a Victorian build- ing on the south side—where Whistler had his account. The original building was by Robert Adam, and when it was demolished in the nineteenth century, the fossils were found in the London clay—the fossil bones of lions, cave bears and tigers who came to drink at the watercourse which flowed towards the Thames in some interglacial epoch in the early days of creation. What is more, those springs still flow under the square, and I believe feed the artesian wells that supply water to the fountains.

It is not wise to dwell on the significance of these things. It is better to be like a friend of mine who has a fossil—a trilobite or an ammonite, I forget which—on his desk in Bloomsbury; when I reminded him that a character in one of Oliver Wendell Holmes's books kept one in similar circumstances, mainly as a reminder of the transcient nature of human life, he said yes, you could use it for that pur- pose, certainly, but he, for his part, only kept it as a paper-weight to stop urgent memoranda from being blown off his desk.

The lions—Landseer's lions on the radial pedestals at the foot of the Nelson Column designed by William Railton—were supposed to symbolise the strength and courage of the British people. To me, they are too docile—though this lack of aggressiveness may make them more expressive of the British as they are today than as they were at the time of erection. Nonetheless, there is very little of the true leonine qualities about them: a lion, even in repose (unless absolutely asleep) rarely fails to convey an impression of watchful energy—a sheer brute strength tempered by magnanimity and disdain—his indolence is not to be counted upon. Landseer's lions are well fed and affable. In a word, they are civic lions of the sort the Victorians dotted up and down the country on the outside of their classic town halls. Landseer's came after a dispute over the four stone ones carved by Thomas Milnes which were originally commissioned. Sir Titus Salt bought the rejected lions, and they have spent the last century in obscurity in the village of Saltaire in Yorkshire.

William IV Street, at the back of the delightful Regency block in the style of Decimus Burton, has a café I visit fairly regularly for its old-fashioned counter and display of Staffordshire groups and Oxo beakers, as much as for its Cadbury mirror advertisement and old-fashioned comfortable service, and a favourite pub of mine, the Final. There is also the interesting Victorian shop of the gunsmiths, Thomas Bland—rich with carving, ironwork and coats-of-arms on the doors—a shop for gentlemen, belonging spiritually to Bond Street or Mayfair, with an atmosphere pertaining to the novels of Anthony Trollope.

The Final is a place of turned mahogany, gold lettered mirrors and stained glass. The saloon has a mosaic floor to cool your feet, and a brass rail to rest them on when you are called to the bar. Best of all, perhaps, is the Schweppes advert for soda water and dry ginger ale, with an Edwardian nymph—the kind of female that Albert Moore painted—at a spring. Watching her from the opposite wall is a group of natty, whiskery gents in titfers, cokes and billycocks, with their day's shoot at their feet. I rate the Final almost as highly as Mooney's Irish House in the Strand a few yards away—the place to recuperate in after a day's Ulysses-like wandering. Upright drinking, talk, stout, Irish whiskey, Sweet Afton cigarettes and crab sandwiches are features of the place, which belongs to the Dublin of the late Victorian age. I hope the forthcoming renovations will not destroy Mooney's character.

On the island—the gents and ladies island—opposite the Garrick Theatre are a couple of Victorian lamps, no longer gas, one of which is very rich. This, the largest, forms a suitably Baroque introduction to the delights of Charing Cross Road, especially as you surface from the gents and view the perspective in the framework of cast-iron leaves, winged consoles and arabesque ornament that forms the base of the three-branched, Corinthian style column of the lamp.

Charing Cross Road, a Victorian canyon, appeals to me for its variegated qualities, with its Villiers Street edginess predominant. The ballyhoo of Tin Pan Alley and its musical instrument shops and jazz record shops may have something to do with it, and so might the shops where you can buy swish clothes, but the Certificate X cinemas (page 8), neon-lit and offering relief from the seven-year itch, have the off-key flavour in the fullest measure. Some years ago, when there were more of them, occupying the façades above the shops, I used to go to Charing Cross Road simply to stare at the Damaroids adverts: 'Damaroids, the Great Rejuvenator'. Now I concentrate on the contents of the windows, relishing the literature especially, and, incidentally, wondering who buys *Self-Flagellation* by Dr Birch and those other learned commentaries, for they never appear to change from one year's end to another. Still, they do sell and well. One of them is by a

friend of mine, an eminent psychiatrist. He wrote it years ago, as a potboiler, under a pseudonym. He was just married to a charming foreign girl, whose knowledge of English was at that time incomplete. She was also more loyal than discreet, for she made a point of staring in all the French-letter shops for her husband's book. When she saw it, she would exclaim 'Nice shop', in delight—a move calculated to knock them even in Villiers Street, let alone the Charing Cross Road.

The clientèle of these establishments (Villiers Street, Edgware Road and Charing Cross Road share most of the really attractive birth-control shops among them) are somewhat shy and inclined to sidle and slither in and out of the door; only those who are after rupture appliances and the like really tread firmly, and even they are sometimes sheepish and act as if they wouldn't know a French letter from a finger stall. Asiatics are, however, completely self-assured. I know this, for I used to know a woman who kept a couple of these emporiums. I would

84

sit and eat queen cakes with her in the back parlour, while the customers were dropping in for rejuvenators and their opposite numbers, the female pills. (That was a great loss to Islington, by the way—the removal of the enamel advert for female pills, manufactured 'under Royal letters patent' when the birth control shop on the Green packed up). One of the richest features of birth control is missing in these days—at least I never see it—and that is the showcard of a bulldog with one end of a French letter in his teeth, the other end being held down by his paws, advertising 'The Never-Rip'. Once, when I asked a qualified friend if this claim were true, he said he didn't know—he'd never kept a bulldog.

These shops, insignificant architecturally but casting a shadow long enough to reach Rome, have an appealing drabness about them: they are rich in the negative qualities found in the coloured working men's clubs of Paddington and the East End, in the run down dining-rooms where old codgers wash away the leaden hours with milky tea—in all places where inadequacy is sought after for its own sake. This suggests that birth control shops have been insufficiently investigated by those in search of new sensations: assuredly there is much more artistic material, in the shape of films, plays and paintings, to be got out of them than has hitherto appeared.

Eventually, the Charing Cross Road area will be spoiled by developments such as the skyscraper block at St Giles's Circus. Meanwhile, the whole length from the island before mentioned up to Tin Pan Alley remains wonderfully intact, the best part of it being Cambridge Circus—a riot of late Victorian aimless ornament with the ironwork of the lavatory acting as a hub (opposite)—Soho bursting out of its boundaries at the North-West corner and Seven Dials at the South-East, edging in by way of the pocket-sized market in Earlham Street, by the Marquis of Granby.

During the war, the lavatory (entirely without interest inside despite the curlicue ironwork above ground) seemed no more than a club for American servicemen—a kind of outpost of that dreadful stage-door canteen in Piccadilly. There is, as a matter of fact, an informal club—a club with advantages over the rest in having no subscriptions to pay and no rules to observe—that meets in the attendant's tiled room in a lavatory off one of the old London squares. I am somewhat of an honorary member, the rest being old men who read their days away in libraries, sleep on benches in the summer or perhaps pick up a trifle by going errands. The nearest they have to a chairman is the attendant, and they know his position in life, as a man holding public office, calls for respect. They sit round the gas-fire, warming their hands or blowing hard on the tea in their saucers (they like their tea well blown at the club), and, like the patrons of the Camden coffee stall, they discuss the merits of the different brands: some are for Mazawattee or Lyons Quick Brew, others weigh in strongly with the qualities of Brooke Bond or the C.W.S. Sometimes the chairman will talk politics to them or show them the latest public health poster he has received for display on the walls or he will talk cisterns to them.

This hobby of his is curious and worth mentioning. He collects lavatory cisterns—not the objects themselves, but the names their makers have bestowed upon them. Down the years, he has made a point of studying them closely, as part of his professional interests, and transcribing their names and other details in a pocket book. He reads out extracts from this book from time to time, mainly in winter when the tea is finished and the members are gathered round the fire. Evidently he finds this a source of satisfaction: I cannot speak for the other members, but his pastime is certainly much to my taste. 'The New Niagara' is one of his prize specimens, then there is 'The Thunderer' and 'The Invincible'; most are London-gathered, since that is where the chairman-attendant has spent his life though the best was collected in Wales on the only holiday he ever had; 'The Dauntless Dolphin'.

To return to Charing Cross Road. The Irving statue (on the site of which some of the best West End mountebanks and street entertainers once performed) is a good point of departure for an exploration of some of the tributary streets. There are pavement artists on this spot today—some of them young, but there is also a veteran who specialises in highly detailed, highly coloured romantic landscapes—thatched cottages, bridges over streams, the true, traditional pavement picture.

Orange Street contains the rough stuccoed Edwardian classic building that was once Ciro's ('We dine at Ciro's, but her Mother comes too'): no table d'hôte, but dinner chosen from an elaborate menu at a guinea, or a less ambitious one at twelve-and-six in those dead, delicious days: and next to it, the tiny Congregational Church, like a country chapel of the Countess of Huntingdon's connection come to town. Whitcomb Street has still the character of a village street about it. At the Pall Mall corner is a wine merchant's with ancient cellars—a labyrinth of old brick arches. When my drawing of these appeared in the Peterborough column of the *Daily Telegraph*, a reader commented that at one time a passage connected these cellars to St James's Palace, and that when he was employed in the wine cellars in the 'nineties, the entrance to this passage could still be seen. There is a barber's, an antique, junk and book shop, several caffs and newsagents— Whitcomb Street is very self-contained.

Excel Court is a curious, crooked, little place, into which the sun manages to get in the afternoon, making geometrical shadows across the stone-flagged pavement and on to the old, peeling, stucco walls. A couple of gas lamps, several dustbins, a pair of coal holes, a small club and the 'Coffee An'' furnish one side, and on the opposite is a mid-nineteenth-century building with a shapely bracketed door. Before the garage arrived, there used to be an ancient caff that I rated highly, with marble-topped tables, greenery-yellowy walls lined with fly-blown mirrors, gas brackets, at the upper or Leicester Square end of Whitcomb Street. Apart from the office girls, who came for take-away sandwiches, the clientèle were mainly oldish men who hadn't yet been pensioned off by their

86

firms and were given to wearing grey mufflers and avoiding draughts. If I opened a boutique, it would be for the benefit of such as these. The very opposite of swinging, its seed-cake character would be marked by the name I should give to it: The Old Square. I should sell patent-leather boots, leggings, mittens, button-hooks, herbal ointments, glass fly-catchers (the ones you fill with a solution of sugar and vinegar), rubber sheets for the incontinent, hair restorer, spats and biscuit barrels; for the women, I should stock curious undergarments, old-fashioned print aprons, cumbersome carpet sweepers, knife-cleaning boards, buttoned shoes, records of the J. H. Squire Celeste Octet, grate polish, vintage gas cookers and dream books.

The Hand and Racquet is Whitcomb Street's local, and rather fine it is, being Victorian pub architecture of some quality. It is an early type, belonging to the period between the gin palace and the full blooded, late Victorian pub (such as the Salisbury). It has the interest of being a dated example, having the year of its erection, 1865, in raised figures on the corner of the façade.

This brings us, for a moment, to Leicester Square, on which an entire book, or indeed a shelf of them, could be written. Architecturally, it is, of course, no longer distinguished. It is the crowds—some of them prime examples of London's fruit and nut cases—tramps, lovers, foreigners, wise guys, bums and the rest—that we look for in Leicester Square. Visitors make extensive use of the benches under the plane trees in the warm weather, to rest their protesting feet, while the pigeons make love among the summer bedding plants. Vinos, junkies and the so-called misfits also come to rest on the benches, having stowed away the empties underneath: in fact, if you wish to have a brief introduction to London's dead-beat population, Leicester Square will almost certainly provide it. A representative selection of the diminishing number of street entertainers show up to beguile the cinema queues on Saturday and Sunday evenings, especially, and there are the odd or bizarre ones who want to put themselves over big for some reason. In recent months, there has been a man in a cocked hat, wig, eighteenth-century costume of grey silk and a chef's check trousers worn under a black cape, looking like one of the impoverished French noblemen who appear in the London of *A Tale of Two Cities*. He stands and eats peanuts, and allows the girls to photograph him. He isn't promoting anything—it is simply his humour to dress up this way, before he goes on the Square to do his tap dance. His name is Lord Mustard.

Though the fine original ironwork, as elaborate as lace, has been replaced by dull modern work on the corner lavatory, the wooden cabman's shelter still lends a late nineteenth-century touch to the N.E. corner of the square. It is not generally realised that most of the modern taxi-cab ranks are only those once occupied by the hansoms or the hackney coach stands; in general, the sites are the same, though the vehicles have changed. Quite a few of these shelters are left in London, in such places as Clapham Common (this being provided by Frederick Gorringe, the draper), Kensington Gore, Hanover Square and St John's Wood.

June, 1967 saw the Diamond Jubilee of *The Merry Widow*: it was at Daly's Theatre in Leicester Square (the Warner Theatre now occupies the site) that Lehar's operetta began its history-making run on a June night in 1907, with Lily Elsie in the title role. The piece was undoubtedly one of those things that occur in art from time to time, in which ordinary people find a magical release, though the art may be of a minor or lightweight character. There can be no precise analysis of the conditions which give rise to this: the same faery tale, frothy, Ruritanian ingredients may be put together and indeed were, even by Lehar himself, without the transformation taking place.

On the East side, the Odeon cinema stands on the site of the Alhambra, a West End music hall where Leotard, the original of the man on the Flying Trapeze in George Leybourne's song, floated with the greatest of ease above the patrons eating and drinking at the marble-topped tables. Max Miller was the last artiste to perform there. When I was recording the demolition of Chelsea Palace, the foreman told me he was 'on the Alhambra job', and that the Cheeky Chappie had turned up among the debris avowing that it was his ambition to be the last artiste to appear at the Alhambra. Therefore, he distributed a fiver among the men who formed themselves into an audience, and Miller entertained them from the ruined stage with half an hour's patter.

Lisle Street and, more particularly, Gerrard Street belong, if not precisely to switched on London, at least to the instant, synthetic-fun London, and they are on the edge of the strip club belt. Lisle Street, once a prostitute's parade ground, has some of its eighteenth-century property left. There are three-bow windowed shops, of which the two best are Smith's, the radio component shop (shops selling wireless parts are a feature of Lisle Street), and Richard's, the dairy next door; the windows have a subtle, shallow curve with a delicate dentil moulding.

Gerrard Street is mostly music shops, jazz clubs and jazz posters: it has that slippery, dislocated air about it I find so satisfactory. But the only building of any real quality is the Boulogne, one of the few genuine Victorian restaurants left in London. The interior, later than the façade, has white walls, mirrors, columns and a row of private boxes at the far end (opposite). Here, as at Rules, you step back into the London of Wilde and Beardsley. Next to it and turning the corner into Wardour Street is one of my favourite London buildings, once Maxim's Chinese Restaurant and now a steak house. The old lincrusta, stained glass and elaborate plaster work were being ripped out as I made my illustration (page 81): it was the end of an era.

In its original condition, Maxim's was an Edwardian extravaganza of 1909— particularly right for the corner of Gerrard Street and Wardour Street. There was a touch of the late 1920s in the scalloped-edged canopy, with the name of the restaurant in red glass and the word 'suppers' below; an attempt in the Wooster period to give a modern face lift to what had by then become an unfashionable façade. The walls above were of cream-painted stucco, with the mouldings picked

out in pale blue, vivid green and scarlet. The time came when Maxim's closed, and the dust began to gather on the rich, old-fashioned décor, as it had gathered over a decade before on the Turkish alcoves of Romano's, and the ground floor began to be covered over with brightly coloured jazz posters—themselves peculiarly right for Wardour Street—and then the end was in sight. As I made the drawing, I reflected how often I had been in at the death of Victorian restaurants and tearooms—Slaters in Piccadilly, where one used to sit in basket chairs, the Kardomah's art nouveau, arts-and-crafts tearoom in Eastcheap, the Holborn Restaurant (most unnerving was my last visit there; I had the place almost to myself under the surveillance of a group of melancholy waiters, as I munched away beneath that splendid mosaic ceiling), Romano's, the Trocadero, the Café Monico and all the rest.

The area of Gerrard, Wardour and Lisle Streets plays an important part in Fletcher's London. It is jazz, neon lit, birth controlled and slightly edgy. The air is perfumed with the perpetual smell of frying ham and steak burgers in the cafés. Sexy books, infinitely less shocking than their covers suggest, are bought, sold and exchanged: non-stop strip,is a speciality. Up and down parade the scenesmen —the youths in sideburns and Carnaby Street-inspired clothes, whose ambition is to stay on the scene—accompanied by kinky dames with hair dyed in unbelievable tints, painted eyes and the shortest skirts in London, the real swinging dolls. There are wandering and wondering provincials (not so far out of their depth either for Wardour Street has an unmistakable Blackpool flavour), shuffling old men who fish things up out of the gutters and waste bins and a heady mixture of all the races on earth.

Wardour Street conditions one for Soho, an area that cannot be dealt with properly, except at length, but a few dislocated observations are, I think, required. But first, if the day be a weekday, visit the market in Rupert Street on the other side of Shaftesbury Avenue. For some reason, the stalls here seem to be more brightly lit and to have fruit and vegetables of larger size and richer colours than any other street market. Flowers, fruit and vegetables are the main interest of Rupert Street, though there is a book stall, and behind the stalls are some very interesting shops—one specialising in spices, another ironmongery, another baskets and one offering Chinese goods.

At the top is Brewer Street. Before turning left to plunge into darkest Soho, take time off to look at Randall and Aubin's. It offers the delightful experience of walking into a complete French shop, though only a stone's throw from Piccadilly. Established in 1906, it was originally a charcuterie and boucherie, though curiously enough with wines as a sideline, a left-over from an earlier occupier, Sir Thomas Lipton. All the meat is still prepared the French way—with the fat and nerves removed to avoid waste. Other specialities of the house include various kinds of patés, fresh snails and frogs' legs, smoked eel and trout, fruits and herbs, bread and confectionery. Even the notepaper is wonderfully period—full of the medals the firm has been awarded, surrounded by lots of decorative engraving. Once you are through the narrow double doors of the shop, you find yourself in an almost perfect interior (the only jarring note being the modern cash register and this can be overlooked), architecturally as agreeable to the connoisseur of shops as its display of foodstuffs is to the gourmet. What's more, all sorts of old Italian and French women drop in, and order what they want in their own language, for they speak all three at Randall and Aubin's, the third, of course, being Cockney.

A dalliance in Soho is always rewarding—a mere loitering with no intent, up and down the quarter, taking in its peculiar atmosphere, under the gaze of the few remaining shady ladies—or, at least, those few who consent to appear. There are three things that can be said about Soho. First, that the observation made (I think) by Max Beerbohm that whereas in the West End you are charged less than you had imagined, in Soho you are charged more than you had supposed is no longer true: the fact is that everything in London is very expensive—sometimes monstrously so—and Soho is no longer dearer, generally speaking, than anywhere else. Second, there are far too many demolitions going on (Bateman's Buildings, at the time I write this), and if they continue unabated, they will destroy the place absolutely; and third that, though neon-lit, slippery Soho is very attractive to me (and I hope to the readers of these pages), the other side of Soho—the eighteenth-century Soho of Dr Manette and his fellow emigrés—deserves more attention as something apart from the restaurants, peep clubs and what not that constitute the main attractions of the district. It is at least as interesting as the Soho of Jack Spot.

The important thing is to have a definite programme, for the air is warm and sluggish there most afternoons in the season when visitors tend to gravitate to Soho; fatigue and a sense of dislocation soon set in if you are wandering aimlessly. You might find your hands and feet swelling under the gaze of the layabouts and unsatisfactory characters who prop themselves up at strategic points, feel disintegration coming on and give in to the invitation shouted down to you by some old bag from an upper window.

Considerable fragments remain of eighteenth-century Soho. There is, for example, the double-fronted eighteenth-century shop with rococo decoration, Rippon's, the newsagent's and tobacconist's, in Dean Street. This is one of the half-dozen fine shops of the Georgian period that have managed to survive. Rippon's is in a block of largely eighteenth-century date: see also St Anne's Court nearby (old houses, dirty books and peep clubs) and, more especially, the stately old houses tucked away in Richmond Buildings. While on the subject of shops, I should mention Hopkins, Purvis and Sons, the colour grinders and oil and varnish merchants, in Greek Street—an entirely delightful early nineteenth-century exterior, complete with a small crane swung back to form a positive item of decoration to the façade.

In Soho Square is the House of St Barnabas, formerly the House of Charity, with a magnificent staircase, panelled rooms and superb plaster work (next page). Permission to see the house is readily given by the charity, by the simple process of knocking at the door and asking; and you can then pass through the rooms where the women inmates are sitting about in easy chairs to see the diminutive chapel in the French Gothic style on the site of Dr Manette's house. The exterior of this chapel, one of the most attractive specimens of Victorian Gothic in London, can be seen as you return to Charing Cross Road by way of Manette Street.

Most of the eighteenth-century houses of Soho are in multi-occupation, with all sorts and conditions of men and women living in well-proportioned, though shabby, old rooms. For that matter, Soho itself is a classic example of multi-occupation—horizontally and vertically: a cellar may be a clip joint, the shop on the ground floor a continental hair stylists, perhaps with a non-stop striptease in

the back room (fifteen gorgeous girls dancing absolutely naked—stay as long as you like—the show's on now) a seedy little office on the floor above and a ponce in the attic. And so on, down the street.

One of the most interesting of the large mansions of the early eighteenth century is No. 76 Dean Street. There are others of similar character, though so entirely chewed up by the restaurants and clubs that have found their way into them, like grubs in an apple, that little of the original interiors are left. No. 76, however, although occupied by a number of business firms, has not been ruined in the process; what gives the house its special distinction is the substantial staircase and old mural paintings of marine subjects on the staircase walls.

The Manor House in Soho Square and the Parish Church of St Anne, together with the old-established shops and the market stalls, are indications—survivals if you like—of the former village of Soho, once on the edge of the fields. Little of that now remains, but people sometimes try to put this across. The film, *Miracle in Soho* (film-makers are now themselves 'villagers' of long standing), was a somewhat corny attempt in this direction: everybody seemed to know everybody else, and to be bursting at the seams with bonhomie; the heroine fell in love with a handsome road mender, whose firm were at work in Soho for a short period, during which the affair progressed seasonably. In order to bring things to a head, she lit a candle and prayed to the Virgin for assistance, and, sure enough, the newly tarmac-ed street sprang a leak, the job had to be redone and they all lived happily ever after—as they always do, in Soho. Then there was *The Doctor in Bean Street*—an altruistic medico kept continually on the hop by the lyings-in, the goings-on and the passings-out of the local rustics, most of whom seemed to revere his name while failing to line his pocket.

There may be this close-knit cameraderie in Soho; if so, I have never noticed it, in spite of many days and nights spent perambulating its precincts. My impression is that the denizens of Soho—both those who live there and those who only go there to work or otherwise occupy their time—are chiefly remarkable for minding their own business. Though it has many occupations, Soho's chief industry is the catering trade—the restaurants, cafés, drinking clubs and those who supply them. In my time I have sampled a very fair cross-section of the Soho eating places, and had a number of strange encounters in them.

One I remember particularly concerns a restaurant now defunct (Soho restaurants—the less successful ones—have a fairly high mortality rate: even the professional skill of the doctor in Bean Street can't save them). It had an encouragingly English name—no foreign nonsense about it. I went often, too often, when I was a Slade student. One night, I went in search of the gent's, which was below stairs. Somehow I went wrong, and wandered in a maze of passages, to come up against a door with lights and voices behind opaque glass. Those voices belonged to a number of gentlemen from an Eastern European country—often known as a foreign power; the whole place, as a view through the keyhole confirmed, reeked with schemes and diablerie. The entire set-up had a strong resemblance to a set for a spy film of the pre-Bond era, in which all the foreigners spoke guttural English and expensive vamps in officer-type macs got up to no good on the Blue Train. Of course, I did nothing about it. I knew no one would believe me, and that, if they did, the place would be empty when the coppers arrived. But one day the police turned up at the Slade and interviewed all those students who had been there, and then I knew that my imagination was not so inflamed as I had hoped. Shortly afterwards the restaurant folded up. That is all I ever knew, except that the chef could make lemon meringue like nobody's business.

Soho Square, if one can resign oneself to the half-timbered, Walt Disney style gardener's hut in the centre, is an agreeable place to lounge in, after trapesing the streets of the quarter. A few old people from the Soho tenements dream in the sun, and there are usually a few children and a sprinkling of layabouts (though fewer now than a year or so ago) to liven things up, and the lawns, trees and flower beds are well cared for. Quite a few of the old houses remain in the square, and there are several interesting buildings such as the French church. L'Eglise Protestante Francaise de Londres (I always think there is something especially admirable about French, Spanish or Italian Protestants) has been in Soho Square since 1893, though the church dates back to 1550 when it was founded by the Huguenot refugees to whom Edward VI granted a charter. To the present day newly appointed pasteurs receive assent from the Sovereign. The present church, in terra cotta, is a pleasing design by Sir Aston Webb, an architect with whose work—the Victoria and Albert Museum, for example—I have usually very little sympathy; it contains a library of rare books and manuscripts.

Lastly, there are two cafés in the area which ought not to be omitted by collectors of the off-beat and full flavoured. The first is the little Welsh dairy in Silver Place, a narrow alley which is a prolongation of Beak Street. It appears to have been lifted bodily from any small Welsh town, such as Lampeter, and it ought to have been written up by Dylan Thomas. The entire alley is a Victorian curiosity, with the dairy as Exhibit A. On the outside, a sign offers 'Light Refreshments'. Inside are two tiny dining-rooms—the one in the shop part is my favourite, where you can sit at marble topped tables and enjoy the conversation as the locals drop in for milk, bread, eggs out of a wicker basket or sandwiches. The shop is equipped with an old-fashioned counter, bent-wood chairs and old biscuit adverts. It is an absolutely ideal place in which to unwind, and the 'light refreshments' are of the best quality. I like to sit there and think of *Under Milk Wood*, of the policeman who used his helmet as a jerry and of a certain Welsh nut-case I often meet, who was a miserable sinner until God leaned out of a cloud and told him so.

The other café of rare delight is at No. 40 Frith Street, almost as good in its fin-de-siècle way as the St Gothard Café in Fulham Road, and like it, putting you back where you belong—the turn of the century—and affording a welcome change from too close a study of vital statistics in Soho's dirty-book, strip-club belt.

94

XI

In the Gothic Manner

———— ✳ ————

APART FROM HAUNTING BILLIARD SALOONS, dingy cafés, Victorian tearooms and pubs, there are few things in Fletcher's London more rewarding than a study of its Victorian Gothic remains. These are fairly evenly distributed over the entire London area, so there is no difficulty in putting together a scientifically balanced, à la carte menu. In the last chapter, I have already mentioned a delectable item—the two bay chapel of Joseph Clarke in the 'French Gothic style' in the garden with the mulberry tree behind the House of St Barnabas in Greek Street, Soho. Examples of Victorian Gothic are likewise to be found in all areas mentioned in this book, with St Pancras Station as the high water mark.

The best of them—there are, of course, many lifeless, mediocre nineteenth-century Gothic buildings all over London—possess, besides their formal, purely architectural qualities which set them apart from the rest, a fervour and a vitality that is still active—like a handful of radiant coals among ashes, compelling us to feel, at least for a moment, something of that idealism that found its romantic outlet in revived Gothic forms. As students of the movement know, Gothic Revival began at least as early as the eighteenth century as one of the several styles the eighteenth century, firmly committed to the classical tradition, was toying with, without any serious intention: Pugin's belief that the Gothic style was the only possible one for Christians to build in would have been totally inconceivable in the eighteenth century. Horace Walpole, a dilettante of influence, was one of the first to make the Gothic manner—as it then was—fashionable, and

it was not long before Gothic details began to creep into the pattern books published by architects, builders and carpenters.

Walpole's house at Strawberry Hill, Twickenham, now a Roman Catholic convent, remains much as he left it; a Gothic toy, yet foreshadowing the shape of things to come, even though entirely free from any suggestion of architectural crusading, much less the moral fervour that gradually became a feature of the movement as ancient Gothic forms were more closely studied and seriously analysed, and as the Romantic movement to which the Revival was linked acquired momentum.

Examples of early or eighteenth-century Gothic are somewhat inaccessible in London, but there are two that can be taken as generally representative—the Gothic front of the Guildhall by George Dance and the charming doorway in Staple Inn, Holborn. Wren's Gothic churches, built to satisfy the desire of those City parishes which, having lost their ancient churches in the Fire, were conservatively minded and averse to a total break from tradition should also be studied, though their influence on the revival was slight. Wren himself had no interest in the Gothic style, though he could perform very adroitly in it, when minded to do so, as can be seen from the interior of St Mary Aldermary with its rich, rather rococo or wedding cake fan vaulting carried out in plaster and the fine nave arcade, above which are spandrils filled with ornament that has almost the character of Art Nouveau, and also from other specimens of his Gothic work— the spire of St Dunstan in the East, which is as romantic as that grave, lofty and practical genius could permit—but it is Gothic that comes from the head, intellectually rather than passionately conceived, and without the passion and belief, revived Gothic is nothing. Although there must have been masons and carvers more accustomed to Gothic forms than to Renaissance ones in the time of Wren (for real Gothic churches continued to be built or repaired in various parts of the country throughout this period, simply because that was the way they had been done for generations) he seems not to have employed them: Wren's Gothic detail is nearly always debased, and very often stodgy. Nonetheless, the City would be infinitely poorer without these Gothic essays by Wren, for though the detail may be coarse and unconvincing, Wren's Gothic churches in the mass are very satisfactory, if inclined to a formality unknown to the Middle Ages, and in the whole corpus of Wren's work, they have, in fact, received insufficient appreciation.

Early Gothic Revival is at its best in minor things, such as doors, lamps and shopfronts. The pump in Grays Inn Square (opposite), still in use, is a very delightful example of this sort of thing, and with it may be classed the Gothic iron balconies of the 1830s—they were not what Pugin meant in his books of architectural polemics and did, in fact, enrage him, but they are charming for all that. Later ironwork of the Revival was, of course, meant to be taken seriously, and there is a lot of it in London—in the Palace of Westminster, all of it designed by Pugin— in the various churches, especially those of the 1860s—it flickers along the tops of roofs and appears in the cast-iron railings of the old suburban terraces and in the pubs, also against the rules. Ruskin, Pugin, Scott and other architectural writers argued for the entire suitability of Gothic shapes for all manner of buildings, and the minor architects and designers, ready then as now to follow fashion, took them at their word and applied it, delightfully debased sometimes, to all sorts of surprising uses—purposes that were considered inadmissible at the time, but are now seen to have led to some of the most attractive examples of Gothic.

One of the most striking is the Star of the East, the great Ruskinian Venetian Gothic pub, with its own private street lamps, in Limehouse. Stand on the traffic island and get the late nineteenth-century lavatory ironwork in the foreground, for the best effect; the sunlight picks out the details of the carved heads of kings and queens, the quatrefoil ornament, pointed arches, the red brick, stamped tile and glass engraved with stars, so that the effect is akin to looking at a Victorian Gothic architect's drawing of an elevation—highly detailed, bright, ineffably romantic and persuasive. You feel it was a good idea of the Victorians to position Gothic buildings all over the East End, as indeed it was—the most magnificent, and the most grievous loss, being the Columbia Market, a kind of St Chapelle dropped into Bethnal Green, of which only a gatepost or two and some of the ironwork now remains.

The Star of the East is a serious and successful attempt at applying Gothic principles to a pub: often enough the Gothic element was merely a soupçon, applied to a design of mongrel or doubtful origin; nevertheless, even in these unpromising circumstances, the Gothic element gives character and vitality, and, anyway, no one can reasonably quarrel with the Victorian pub architects, even at their wildest, for they knew their business thoroughly, and produced pubs that have never been equalled for effectiveness. My illustrations of the Albert in Victoria Street (opposite) and of the iron finial of the Jolly Butchers (Page 100). show typical examples of this infiltration of Gothic details into a non Gothic design. The Albert has a curiously nineteenth-century American-like exterior, and the balconies are quite superb.

In Stoke Newington, besides the fantastic Gothic ironwork of the Jolly Butchers (the honeysuckle ornament of the cornice is also cast iron), the Gothic Revival may be studied in the huge Victorian church by Scott, opposite the ancient parish church of the former village. Scott's spire has a good deal in common with the spire of his church of St Mary Abbots, Kensington. The latter was dedicated in 1872, the spire being completed in 1879. Here again appear the Early English details—for instance, the West door—that Scott utilised so frequently, and the piers, alternately octagonal and quatrefoil, that are also a favourite motif. As elsewhere, the exterior elevations are much more satisfactory than the interior (the most successful feature of all being perhaps the cloister added much later in the 'nineties), for, although the general effect, particularly of the six bay nave arcade and triforium—is irreproachable, the details are mechanical and dis-

appointing, as was so often the case with Scott.

Although he had an immense experience as a church architect, Scott could seldom or never infuse into his ecclesiastical work the vitality and, as it were, belief that Street and the more angular and uncompromising Butterfield got into theirs; he remains the true academic, with a complete command over the language but with nothing to say. Altogether Scott presents a problem: he did too much, for one thing; his talents lay in the direction of administration and organisation, for another; and he was a populariser rather than a creative artist. As far as my knowledge goes, at no time did Scott build a church so truly romantic and beautiful as St Luke's, Chelsea (by James Savage)—quite one of the most perfect, as well as one of the earliest nineteenth-century Gothic churches of London, and I am thinking of Scott's many provincial designs, including his most attractive church at Worsley, near Manchester. Yet Scott could bring an unlooked for fervour, and impart an almost exalted quality to a railway station. That is what is so baffling.

Ironwork on facade
of the Jolly Butchers
Stoke Newington

As a Gothic apologist, Scott is worth reading, and contrasts with Pugin's fervid eloquence much in the way an informed, well-bred man might do, talking reasonably at his club, with a Hyde Park orator. Scott's architecture is, in fact, well bred, though this is really not the cause of its negative qualities; these arise out of a fundamental low temperature, an artistic anaemia, combined with mass production . . . 'a gross of kings', as Ruskin said, 'sent down from Kensington'.

This Kensington Gothic reaches its climax in the Albert Memorial, a contrivance I have never commented on at length, hitherto, partly because it has received a good deal of attention in recent years and partly because it is what horticulturalists term a 'sport'. Once it was laughed at and became every fool's symbol for summing up Victorian taste. Since then, it has been overpraised; the real truth being that, though by no means a monstrosity, it is really no more than an expensive version of Scott's usual Gothic establishment style, with a genteel vulgarity peculiarly its own. Scott's own design was preceded by some months by Worthington's Albert Memorial at Manchester. The Manchester memorial belongs to an earlier Gothic Revival style—the one that produced the Scott Memorial in Edinburgh—whereas Scott's design is High Victorian Gothic. On the whole, Scott's is the more attractive of the two, possibly gaining something from its setting in the park, while Worthington's design loses somewhat by juxtaposition with the Town Hall, the most magnificent large scale building the Gothic Revival produced.

From a distance, in the sunlight, the Albert Memorial is like a jewelled casket (Scott had the idea of a ciborium or medieval shrine in mind) though gone rather dull—like some saint's reliquary, surprisingly rich, found in an obscure French church. The reliquary's top is the spire composed of figures in niches, the jewellery is the mosaic in the triangular pediment, the carved ivory the base of the naturalistic figure sculpture of great artists, composers and architects. The mosaics in the pediment and those of the spandrils of the arch are curiously like the contemporary Arundel Society prints.

At the corners of the monument, the four great groups of figure sculpture representing the continents are intensely Victorian and, like the frieze on the monument itself, in no way Gothic. This is one of the characteristics that give the thing its unique flavour. I like 'Asia' best—the Indian woman on the kneeling elephant, the turbanned figure leaning against the animal's back and the bald heathen Chinese at its side. On the day of my last visit, there actually was a bald, live Chinaman sitting on the step immediately below the figure and making a piquant contrast, for he wasn't looking inscrutable, like the carved Chinaman above, he was looking rather smug, as he smoked his cigarette and drank his bottle of Pepsi-Cola, for you must know that Cathay itself has changed and that the new Yellow Peril consists in the constantly multiplying Chinese Restaurants, even unto Deptford.

After 'Asia', I go for the group symbolising 'America'—a great bison, surrounded by women from the wild woods and a Red Indian brave. Unfortunately, on the other side of the group, there is a ludicrous introduction—a trapper who looks for all the world like General Custer thinking things out at Little Bighorn (complete with hat, long hair and heavy moustache) only—and this is the crumminess of it—wearing considerably less clothes than either a trapper or a general would consider the regular thing; the figure on the bison is, however, very fine.

The frieze, sculpted by J. B. Philip and H. H. Armstead, on the base of the monument, with its figures of architects, artists, composers and writers is a strange enough assembly, though it is well carved and designed. Cockerell and Barry in their nineteenth-century frockcoats and tight trousers seem odd in the company of Wren and Vanbrough in their full-bottomed wigs, and so do Ictinus and Callicrates, the architects of the Parthenon, not to mention the man who built the Pyramids. Pugin appears, a handsome figure and a good likeness, at one of the angles, in the monkish robe he affected, and Scott himself is of the company of immortals—a head in the crowd—more modestly placed than one would have thought possible. Hogarth is there, with his inseparable companion, the artist's pug dog, Pompey, and Turner, with a finger or two chipped off. Finally and above all, the good prince surveys the traffic of Kensington Gore from under his canopy, with nothing more interesting to beguile the years than a copy of the Great Exhibition catalogue.

In all, the Albert Memorial is worth a careful inspection, but more as a curiosity of Victorian taste and optimism than as an example of the smaller monuments of the Gothic Revival. These should be studied in such places as the Embankment Gardens by the Houses of Parliament, where there is an interesting memorial by S. S. Teulon which was once in Parliament Square; Scott's well designed Gothic cross at Charing Cross—as good as his Martyrs Memorial at Oxford; and the Gothic memorial to Tom Smith, the Christmas cracker man, in Finsbury Square.

Teulon made some interesting, if uncomfortable, contributions to the Gothic Revival: his work is at times almost as determinedly personal as Butterfield's, though artistically inferior. Much of it has a French Gothic, or rather French Gothic Revival, flavour: perhaps the best and most acceptable example of his work is the church of St Stephen, Hampstead, a design that owes something of its effect to its site on the slope of Haverstock Hill, but more to the dramatic and original tower, and the treatment of the details is less heavy-handed than is usual in Teulon's designs. There are times—for instance, on a spring evening, when the daylight is fading and the building is lighted inside—that the church becomes almost as strongly evocative in its own way of the period as Butterfield's All Saints, Margaret Street, or Street's St James the Less in Thorndike Street, which, with its gilding, tile and marble and fading mural by G. F. Watts, justifies the comment I have made on it elsewhere—that it is like walking into a Victorian chromolithograph—a feeling that the mid-Victorian age with all its ideals and aspirations is still going on outside.

Those who would study in a brief course the character of Mid-Victorian Gothic in London need do no more than visit St James the Less, St Pancras Station and All Saints to feel the moral fervour and enthusiasm at work to produce an original architecture—not imitative Gothic, as superficial critics once held, but something significant and imaginative, and of the time more truly representative than the Crystal Palace, for the Victorians, however entangled and inconsistent in their thought, were at the bottom fervid idealists more than calculating utilitarians.

This intense feeling communicates itself to us in All Saints. Time has mellowed the determined brutalism of Butterfield's patterns and London smoke the polychromatic colour: from a distance the soaring green spire breaks out of the dull late Victorian and Edwardian stuff that surrounds it, and appeals to the imagination. Close to it is the wonderfully planned courtyard with clergy houses to the right and left, anticipating, though more austerely, Webb and Morris ideas carried out later at the Red House. (Butterfield would never have allowed the picturesque touches and delicate textures of brickwork: in these and other parsonage houses he relies solely on the opposition of masses of wall to deftly placed Gothic windows, uses ordinary red brick and strikes diagonals across it, apparently indifferent to where they are placed, in blue brick, all in an unbending, almost anti-artistic manner.) The interior, full of carved marble, encaustic tile and gilding is like an illuminated book—a Victorian one produced by lithography—and is so evocative of its period that we feel impelled to High Church principles against our judgement and determine on reading Keble and Pusey over again.

Almost equally persuasive is Street's St Mary Magdalen, Paddington. Until a few years ago it stood among decayed nineteenth-century terraces. Now an isolated relic of High Victorian Gothic, it appears uncomfortably among new blocks of flats, like a ship aground, and in the strongest possible contrast to them. The mellow interior, smelling of incense, is full of saints, carved or in stained glass, and there are statues of saints in niches above the springing of the arches of the arcades. The treatment of the two sides of the nave differs. On one side, the arcade is on octagonal columns, the intercolumniation between each being filled by a slender shaft and subarches, and on the opposite side the nave arcade consists of clustered shafts. The materials of the interior are pinkish brick, banded with stone; the barrel roof is richly painted and gilded; the apse is magnificent with marble and gold, with crucifixes, altars and statues: profuse enough but considerably less bizarre than Butterfield's All Saints, and less Ruskinian than Street's previously mentioned church of St James the Less. The two taken together show how gifted, resourceful and inventive Street was. The period flavour is strong: the alms boxes, characteristically Victorian, have quotations from scripture on them. The clock high above in the spire sounds the passing of time; there is rust on the ironwork of the porch and door hinges, and outside the deadend kids are playing in the sun in the concrete dust.

Street's major London building, the Law Courts, although impressive, seems

103

Tower House,
Melbury Road, Kensington

to me (probably because of the confined site and the many conditions imposed on the designer) to lack the unity, as well as the dramatic quality, of Waterhouse's Manchester Town Hall. Waterhouse, himself a competitor for the Law Courts project, hardly appears at his best in either the Natural History Museum or the Prudential, though the recent cleaning which has turned the Pru back into the rose-red citadel the Victorians saw when the building was completed in 1895 has made it somewhat more palatable. The style might be called Insurance Gothic. In passing, the curious may like to be reminded that 'Gothic' lettering is still used in the Law Courts—the notices forbidding cameras are in a Victorian Gothic style, and the telephone boxes in Fleet Street have the word 'Telephones' painted in Lombardic capitals.

At one time, I believed the upsurge of the Gothic Revival to be the result of the propaganda of intellectuals like Ruskin and the insidious, almost unanswerable, arguments of Pugin and those who followed them. But now I see that it can only be explained on the hypothesis that it answered to a need, amounting almost to a hunger, for something beyond experience: at no time since the collapse of the Middle Ages had an expression of this longing been required of architecture. And on the rare occasions when the architecture truly answered to this need, its vitality, as in the churches above mentioned, remains unimpaired. That is what is so touching about them.

Some of the most attractive domestic buildings of the revival are the almshouses the Victorians scattered in the former country areas, such as Penge and Highgate, and also in Metropolitan London: the early nineteenth-century Trinity Almshouses on the riverside at Greenwich are a particularly engaging example of what could be done. I have often congratulated the inmates of such places on their felicity and on the completeness and picturesqueness of their Gothic arrangements, but they are full of woes, indifferent to pointed windows and cast iron Gothic fireplaces, and much given to complaints about their neighbours, especially in the women's almshouses, where each will describe the iniquities of the rest, as if she were not herself a fellow tartar. Gothic domestic architecture, of course, can be studied all over London—the good examples, designed by architects in the exclusive residential areas, the poorer ones, at the other end of the scale, in the form of terraces with Gothic bits tacked on, built by speculative builders.

Examples of Gothic Revival furniture, to be studied in connection with the houses, can be seen at the V and A. Some of the smaller pieces of domestic furniture, more or less Gothic in style, are very attractive, even when by designers of less calibre than Morris or Webb; the cradle by Norman Shaw, for example. The work by William Burges should be noted as showing the kind of interior decoration which went into the house the architect built for himself in Melbury Road, Kensington. Tower House has remained to this day very much as Burges left it, thanks to a succession of enlightened occupiers, just as William Morris's Red House has done, each almost painfully evocative of its period and original owners. Tower House, with its circular, creeper covered turret, is very medieval (opposite): it dates from 1875–80.

In spite of recent intrusions which disrupt the harmony, Melbury Road is a most interesting survival: several of the great Victorian painters, among them G. F. Watts, Luke Fildes and Holman Hunt, lived there and in the immediate area, magnificently housed in the palatial studio mansions built for them by leading nineteenth-century architects. The Gothic Revival was, of course, applied to commercial buildings, sometimes very agreeably, especially in small scale work, such as the warehouse in a mixed Gothic-Romanesque style in Little Britain, from which I illustrate a capital, somewhat in Burges's style (page 95).

The finish and craftsmanship the Victorians put into these buildings is remarkable. There are Gothic blocks in Queen Victoria Street—Manchester in London— bald and produced to recipe; these are of little interest; without doubt, the most

105

successful application of Gothic to commercial use is in the altogether delightful building that used to be the National Bank of Australasia, behind the Bank of England in Lothbury, which embodies all the principles in and lifts some of the details from 'The Stones of Venice'.

Two other late examples of the Revival are worth including. These are Stanhope House (opposite), now mostly occupied by Barclays Bank in Park Lane, and the house built by the Astor family and now used as offices on the Embankment near the Temple. Stanhope House was designed by W. H. Romaine-Walker, a pupil of Street, for Hudson, the soap king. The date of the building, 1898, places it a quarter of a century after the style had reached its peak, but it is a very complete and elaborate example of the Revival: one that combines motifs derived from French Flamboyant Gothic with (particularly in the ironwork) a hint of the contemporary Art Nouveau. The façade remains unaltered. The bank has taken great care to preserve as much as possible of the original interior. The elaborate chandeliers, the magnificent fireplace, with cast-iron back and side panels framed by an ornate overmantel and surround, and the panelling remain intact. Both Stanhope House and the Astor House (by Pearson, 1894) which has a magnificent staircase are choice examples not only of the sumptuous order of life a private individual could achieve in late Victorian London, but also of the craftsmanship still available at a late period.

By the 'nineties, the Revival was at the ebb, and it is interesting to close a brief review by two buildings in which the style is distinctly art nouveau. That Art Nouveau Gothic came into being is not surprising, for among the components of the Art Nouveau style the sinuous Gothic line, derived at a distance through William Morris and certain decorative arrangements by Rossetti and Burne Jones, was as fundamental as the contribution made by the art of Japan.

The Middlesex Guildhall in Parliament Square, built on the site of the ancient sanctuary of Westminster, was opened in 1913. The subtle art nouveau flavour is best seen in the monkish figures which support the balcony on the Abbey side, in the gargoyles and in the shallow arches of the main entrance, where, incidentally, is a quantity of good stone carving depicting incidents in the history of Westminster; but the general character of the building has the distinctively rigid lines characteristic of Art Nouveau in its last phase.

Holy Trinity Church, Sloane Street, is actually more accurately described as Arts and Crafts Gothic, rather than Art Nouveau; the languorousness of curve and ambiguity of feeling characteristic of the latter being only present at Holy Trinity in a subsidiary degree, as in the iron railings by Wilson in Sloane Street outside and the electric light pendants by Sedding, restored and slightly simplified after war damage. The great east window is by Burne-Jones. Morris and his followers were closely associated with the decoration of the building, which is of unique importance because it forms what amounts to a repository of the work of the 'nineties, in which various influences—Sedding's own tendency to Italian idioms,

Arts and Crafts passing into Art Nouveau and late-Pre-Raphaelite-William Morris—are all integrated into a harmonious whole.

Some of the most interesting neo-Gothic buildings in London are the fire stations (though there are a number of Art Nouveau ones, probably the best being the one in the Euston Road by W. E. Riley, 1902). The Bishopsgate Fire Station is my own favourite, but there is an amusing free-style Gothic one in Chiltern Street, Marylebone, of 1889 that comes a close second. The date, with the letters M.F.B. above, occurs in a panel between two mullioned windows surmounted by a flat, ogee, crocketted arch. Besides the date, the panel contains a device of crossed fire axes and a fireman's belt. On each side of the window, flat pinnacles terminate in corbels each carved with a fireman's head. At the fire station doors, through which many a choice horse-drawn turnout must have galloped, are clustered columns and a Gothic observation tower points to the sky above and behind the main block, a symbol of the aspirations of the Victorian medievalists, who set out to create a new and Gothic Jerusalem and almost succeeded.

XII

An Introduction to Fletcher's London

———————— * ————————

AS NO ONE EVER READS INTRODUCTIONS, I have placed this one and its illustrations at the back, so that newcomers to these characteristic samples of the London I prefer will know what they have been reading about.

Fletcher's London, subjected to close scrutiny, will prove to be an elusive thing —one of moods, atmospheres and offbeat sensations. It is certainly no dusty antiquarian affair (though there is, indeed, a case for wishing it were such—a place of old trams, old books, inconceivably antique attitudes, existing largely for hermits who have opted out of the twentieth century) for, though its glances are almost always backward, it can take the surrealist, uneasy atmosphere of Carnaby Street in its stride, and absorb a shop such as Kleptomania in Kingley Street (page 112), where long-haired youths of uncertain sex are trying on secondhand clothes, button boots and granny specs and buying old flat-irons, adverts for pimple removing soap and moustache cups, without a tremor. Everything and anything, provided it be strangely flavoured and out of the way is raw material for its tough uncritical digestion. Each day spent in London by the devotees of the cult yields its harvest of sensations that range from the homely though bizarre to the definitely sinister, the appetite for these things growing with the feeding. As Oscar Wilde said of cigarette smoking, the pleasure lies in the fact that it fails to satisfy.

Yesterday I walked from Limehouse to Aldgate, taking time off now and again to inspect a particularly unpromising street. In one of these, otherwise entirely deserted, I found a discarded perambulator full of helpings of fish and chips, wrapped in newspapers. It summed up Fletcher's London in a stale but powerful symbol. One Sunday in the City, in a desolate landscape of cereal packet office blocks, I found a tramp, the only living person in that forlorn place, barefoot on a step, examining his boots. He looked up at me as I passed, and our eyes met; it was a moment big with futility and emptiness, but neither of us took advantage of it. That again was Fletcher's London.

Café society figures largely in this London—the snack bars where married couples stare around them and at each other, having long exhausted all the conversation possible to them, and caffs, lower down the conventional scale, where old men carry on Mutt and Jeff or Pinter-type conversations, full of repetitions, with no aim except that of killing time. The unbearable monotony, the absolute tedium vitae of all this, is the very essence of connoisseurship. People buy cars nowadays not to get from one place to another, but to make them feel important, to create the illusion of movement, of things happening to them. Addicts of Geoffrey Fletcher's London require no such aids—stimulating arrangements of architecture and people, and flavourful happenings, are going on all the time, and welling up, so to speak, from the centre. Well trained eyes and ears are all that is needed by way of equipment, a Walt Whitman-like relish for the inconceivable variety of metropolitan streets and a like capacity for absorbing it, selecting nothing, rejecting nothing, as the great kaleidescope turns now this way, now that, presenting an endless succession of dissolving views.

Architecturally, one is perhaps better if one refrains from exercising a too critical faculty; in any case, half the charm of offbeat London is in the architecture usually considered to be undistinguished. Take the Michelin Garage (page 111) at the corner of Sloane Avenue and Brompton Road, for instance. It is, of course, late Art Nouveau, and quite superb: it belongs to the days when cars were called motor-cars by everybody except bounders. Now, even bounders have gone, though, like the quack-doctors, they flourish under new names. This is art nouveau passing into George V Classic, with a suggestion of 1920 cinema architecture superadded; the colour scheme is of white tile, with grey and green tiles, and red brick at the sides of the building. Here, perhaps, is its most engaging feature, for what my drawing does not show are the coloured tiled pictures of early motoring events, with conventionalised art nouveau trees and strokes to indicate speed (obviously an early example of the convention) by the side and at the back of the vehicles.

These decorations alone make the garage a fit subject for a pilgrimage, but there are other features of great interest—the two tyres in yellow tile flanking the central window, the tyres surrounded by leaves and berries in the curved pediments and the art nouveau ironwork of the façade. The building is unique, and should be preserved in its entirety (only the present day cars and customers are wrong: they ought, of course, to be encouraged to wear motoring goggles and hobble skirts and to turn up in vintage cars: as they are now they are chronically out of harmony). And though it may not be at once apparent, the Michelin Garage is undoubtedly a tail-end product of the poetic feeling most Victorians had for engineering works—the double vision that enabled them, especially in the early railway age, to conceive utilitarian projects in a romantic spirit. That the Victorians, and even the Edwardians, were able to romanticise commercial buildings proves the persistency, up to a late period, of the English romantic spirit.

Advertising art plays an important part in Fletcher's London; on the one hand, the metal advertisements, signs and shop fascias of the nineteenth century—the period posters such as those for Crufts Dog Show (a magnificent one this, with a woodcut of a St Bernard), for boxing, Chlorodyne, Start Rite shoes, the posters for horror or sex-spectacular films; and on the other, the contrived events of the ad-men, as acceptable to me as genuine, spontaneous events are to normally constituted persons. Verisimilitude to a real happening is, of course, a secondary consideration with me: in fact, the more obviously synthetic, the more I like it. Until the advent of the P.R.O. man with his machinery for making things occur, we were obliged to rely on blind chance or accident; now we can make things happen under controlled conditions, not allowing them to take place until we are ready to cope with them, so imparting balance and harmony and artistic selection to what used to be at best a purely fortuitous process.

With the London-made event as a source of pleasure goes contrived or synthetic fun. Sometimes, as with the May Day procession in Battersea Park, or a special occasion like the Festival of Britain, artificially-inseminated fun (something you normally have to pay for) is provided free as part of an engineered event: I call to mind the Nell Gwynn girls who exposed their bosoms and offered apples for sale at the opening of the Battersea Pleasure Gardens (the elephantine revels of that dreadful Festival were a thing of wonder), the arrival of Father Christmas at any London store, the commercial publicity or official propaganda sneaked into the Lord Mayor's Show and so on. Mostly in London, as elsewhere, you have to pay for ersatz fun—for the fun of being rubbernecked round London's sights, for the fun of the nite spots where they kid you you can take one of the sex kittens home, and beyond it, for the fun of the G-string shows, the bingo palaces, the clip joints, the piped music in pubs.

Among the free examples of fun engineering are the lectures on personality development, the arrival of celebrities, the summer entertainments, including Morris dancing and other wonderfully depressing events, in the London parks, and the pub pancake races of the East End, all of which have the same value as collector's items as had the vanished mock auctions and Japanese atrocity exhibitions of Oxford Street.

Fletcher's London is both old-fashioned and new-fangled. It is a place of a million small, entirely worthless happenings suddenly observed and their flavour extracted on the instant: a priest rolling an eye at a girl's legs, a homosexual wearing make-up seen in a Chelsea shop, a hand chucking away a cola bottle, a fruit and nut case coming up to you in the street to tell you he's just seen Jesus Christ in Rosebery Avenue, an old woman hitting a political poster with an umbrella, an old man staring in the windows of a funeral parlour: all of which items are guaranteed no two alike and genuinely unused.

Fletcher's London is a place where you can still find old-fashioned terraced cottages, with real gardens, surrounded by palings, with window boxes ornamented with miniature wicket gates or encrusted with cork or shells, where they do not have motor bikes, shrouded like phantoms, in the garden; where you can still find hairdressers who call their places saloons, and have not yet given up Lincrusta walls, marble and gold lettering; where single, slightly rum old ladies preside over old-established tearooms, in which the art nouveau decorations have survived time and change long enough to be fashionable once more; where billiard-

Michelin
Tyre Co
Kensington

hall men still have sallow complexions and struggling moustaches, and hope to commit adultery some time.

All-nite, coin-operated laundries, blue-tiled, bagwash laundries, pawnbrokers, body-building gymnasiums, amusement arcades, betting and dirty-book shops, establishments where they sell plastic flowers, artificial grass and ornaments for graves—everything that is clip, kinky, teazy, country fresh though stale and made in town—all these are part of Fletcher's London. In this world, bad pictures and inferior architecture are preferred to the good, just as semblances and imitations are preferred to the real, the container to the contents. It prefers Woolworths to Harridges, the dowdy to the fashionable, failure to success, and it sends old post-cards of Great War camps and Temperance processions to its few friends. The study of it has become a fine art, with its own literature, theories and exponents. Nowadays one encounters visitors intent on seeing the unusual in localities

unheard of, at one time, as tourist haunts. Things that were once unusual are now becoming common-place, merely by being visited: you find visitors intent on seeing second-hand sewing-machine shops, transport cafés, early underground stations with art nouveau decorations on the lifts.

Fortunately London has ample reserves of this off beat material, so connoisseurs have no immediate cause for alarm. Moreover, new possibilities constantly open up. Today, after passing the Victoria Coach Station for years, I have at last become aware of the pure 1930 Blackpool character of it; a quality enriched by the pie-consuming, orange-ade drinking, luggage-lugging customers. Tomorrow it must be examined in depth. . . .